NORMAN THE NEPHITE'S

CHURCH HISTORY

TIME LINE

ILLUSTRATED BY
PAT BAGLEY

WRITTEN BY
WILLIAM W. SLAUGHTER

© 1996 Pat Bagley, William W. Slaughter
All rights reserved. No part of this book may be reproduced in any form or by any means without permission in writing from the publisher, Deseret Book Company, P.O. Box 30178, Salt Lake City, Utah 84130

ISBN 1–57345–195–9   CIP 96–085131
Printed in Hong Kong

10 9 8 7 6 5 4 3 2 1

DESERET BOOK COMPANY
SALT LAKE CITY, UTAH

JOSEPH SMITH (THE RESTORATION BEGINS)

JOSEPH SMITH (1805–1844)

Born on December 23, 1805, in Sharon, Vermont, to Joseph and Lucy Mack Smith, Joseph Smith grew up on a series of tenant farms where he learned the responsibility of hard work. From Vermont the Smiths moved in 1811 to Lebanon, New Hampshire. It was here that Joseph had an operation that saved his leg, but left him with a slight limp. Five years later they moved to Palmyra, New York, relocating two years after that to nearby Manchester. However, he said, "[I was] deprived of . . . education, suffice it to say I was merely instructed in reading, writing, and the ground rules of arithmetic." Nevertheless, his mother said that Joseph was "given to meditation and deep study."

Affected by the great religious excitement taking place around his home in 1820, fourteen-year-old Joseph was determined to know which of the many religions he should join. Obeying the words of James 1:5, he went to a secluded woods and prayed to God for guidance. The Father and the Son appeared to him, telling him to "join none of them, for they were all wrong, . . . 'they draw near to me with their lips, but their hearts are far from me.'" This was the first in a series of events that changed his life as well as religious history.

JOSEPH SMITH SR. (1771–1840)

The father of the Prophet Joseph Smith was born on July 12, 1771, in Topsfield, Massachusetts, to Asael and Mary Smith. He married Lucy Mack on January 24, 1796, in Tunbridge, Vermont. Joseph Sr. trusted and asserted the truth of his son's experiences from the time of the First Vision. Father Smith, as he was known, was one of the Eight Witnesses to the Book of Mormon and was the Church's first patriarch. He died in Nauvoo on September 14, 1840.

LUCY MACK SMITH (1775–1856)

Mother and early biographer of the Prophet Joseph Smith, Lucy Mack was born July 8, 1775, to Solomon and Lydia Mack. Lucy became the mother of nine children who grew to adulthood.

A religious woman whose belief in God was central to her life, Lucy Mack Smith firmly supported her son Joseph's religious teachings. She died on May 14, 1856, in Nauvoo, Illinois.

HYRUM SMITH (1800–1844)

Beloved and trusted by his brother Joseph, Hyrum was one of the Eight Witnesses to the Book of Mormon, a founding member of the Church, a missionary, assistant president of the Church, associate president, and Church patriarch. Of their close relationship the Prophet stated, "I love him with that love, that is stronger than death." Hyrum was martyred with his brother on June 27, 1844.

SAMUEL SMITH (1808–1844)

Samuel Smith was the Church's first missionary and one of the Eight Witnesses to the Book of Mormon. He died July 30, 1844, from a fever caused by injuries sustained while unsuccessfully riding to the aid of Hyrum and Joseph at the Carthage Jail. Samuel's family went west to Utah with the Saints.

WILLIAM SMITH (1811–1893)

A member of the Quorum of Twelve Apostles (1835) and Church patriarch after Hyrum's death, William Smith was the only Smith brother to survive beyond the Nauvoo period. Although loyal to Joseph, he had a contentious spirit, even physically assaulting Joseph in December 1835. He was excommunicated in 1845 after refusing to accept the leadership of the Twelve after Joseph's death. In 1878 he joined the Reorganized Church of Jesus Christ of Latter Day Saints. He died in Iowa in November 1893.

BOOK OF MORMON

MORONI

Moroni survived the battle at Cumorah in A.D. 385 when Lamanite armies wiped out the Nephites. In A.D. 421 he completed and buried the sacred history of the Nephites begun by his father, Mormon. He appeared as an angel to Joseph Smith on September 21, 1823, and told him of the gold plates in the Hill Cumorah (near Palmyra, New York). He instructed Joseph to obtain and translate the record.

HILL CUMORAH, GOLD PLATES

When Joseph Smith went to the Hill Cumorah on September 22, 1823, to get the plates, Moroni told him he wasn't ready. Joseph returned yearly until September 22, 1827, when he was permitted to remove the gold plates from the Hill Cumorah. Having the appearance of gold (they may have been a gold alloy), the plates measured about six inches by eight inches and six inches thick; some who lifted them said they weighed 50 to 60 pounds.

TRANSLATION OF THE BOOK OF MORMON

To help him translate the Book of Mormon, Joseph received a special interpreting instrument called a Urim and Thummim. At various times he was aided by his wife, Emma, Martin Harris, Oliver Cowdery, and a few others, who acted as scribes. As he dictated, his scribes wrote.

From April 12 to June 14, 1828, Martin Harris acted as Joseph's scribe in the translation of the Book of Mormon. Unfortunately, the 116 pages they produced were stolen when Harris took them to show his family. After this incident Harris no longer acted as scribe. The translation progressed slowly until April 5, 1829, when Joseph met Oliver Cowdery, who offered to act as scribe. They began on April 7 and completed the translation by the last week of June 1829. The first edition of the Book of Mormon was printed by Egbert B. Grandin in March 1830.

OLIVER COWDERY (1806–1850)

Born at Wells, Vermont, on October 3, 1806, Oliver Cowdery, a rural schoolteacher, was a scribe to Joseph Smith, one of the Three Witnesses, and associate president of the Church. With Joseph, he experienced many momentous milestones in the restoration of the gospel. Excommunicated on April 12, 1838, he was rebaptized at Council Bluffs, Iowa, in November 1848. He died at Richmond, Missouri, on March 3, 1850.

BOOK OF MORMON WITNESSES

The Three Witnesses. In June 1829 Oliver Cowdery, Martin Harris, and David Whitmer were chosen as special witnesses to the Book of Mormon. The angel Moroni showed them the gold plates, and the voice of God told them the book was divinely translated. The men were allowed to touch, lift, and closely examine the plates.

The Eight Witnesses. A few days later Joseph Smith showed the gold plates to eight others, who were also allowed to handle them. They were Christian Whitmer, Jacob Whitmer, Peter Whitmer Jr., John Whitmer, Hiram Page, Joseph Smith Sr., Hyrum Smith, and Samuel H. Smith.

The testimonies of both sets of witnesses appear in the front pages of the Book of Mormon.

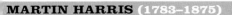

MARTIN HARRIS (1783–1875)

Born in May 1783 in Easton, New York, Martin Harris was a prosperous farmer who was known as industrious, honest, and generous. He was one of the Three Witnesses, and it was his $3,000 that financed the first 5,000 copies of the Book of Mormon.

Harris clashed with Church leaders over monetary practices and was excommunicated in December 1837; he was rebaptized November 7, 1842. He died July 10, 1875, in Clarkston, Utah.

DAVID WHITMER (1805–1888)

One of the Three Witnesses, David Whitmer was born January 7, 1805, to Peter Whitmer Sr. and Mary Whitmer. It was at the Whitmers' Fayette, New York, farm that Joseph Smith was able to complete the Book of Mormon translation. The Church was organized in 1830 at the Whitmer house.

He was excommunicated in April 1838. He died January 25, 1888, in Richmond, Missouri, where he had served on the city council and as mayor.

TESTIMONIES NEVER DENIED

Although all Three Witnesses suffered excommunication (Cowdery and Harris were rebaptized), David Whitmer stated in 1887, "It is recorded . . . that I, David Whitmer, have denied my testimony as one of the three witnesses to the divinity of the Book of Mormon; and that the other two witnesses . . . denied their testimony. . . . I will say once more to all mankind, that I have never at any time denied that testimony or any part thereof. I also testify to the world, that neither Oliver Cowdery or Martin Harris ever at any time denied their testimony. They both died reaffirming the truth of the divine authenticity of the Book of Mormon."

AARONIC PRIESTHOOD

On May 15, 1829, Joseph Smith and Oliver Cowdery prayed about the doctrine of baptism described in the Book of Mormon. John the Baptist appeared in a cloud of light and laid his hands upon their heads, saying, "Upon you my fellow servants, in the name of Messiah I confer the Priesthood of Aaron, which holds the keys of the ministering of angels, and of the Gospel of repentance, and of baptism by immersion for the remission of sins; and this shall never be taken again from the earth, until the sons of Levi do offer again an offering unto the Lord in righteousness."

As instructed by John the Baptist, Joseph and Oliver baptized each other in the Susquehannah River.

MELCHIZEDEK PRIESTHOOD

On the banks of the Susquehannah River, in the summer of 1829, Joseph Smith and Oliver Cowdery received the Melchizedek Priesthood from Peter, James, and John, who also ordained them apostles.

PROPHET, SEER, AND REVELATOR

Today the president of the Church is often referred to as the prophet, seer, and revelator, but this title is associated with apostleship and having received the full "keys of the Melchizedek Priesthood."

On March 27, 1836, at the dedication of the Kirtland Temple, Joseph Smith "called upon . . . the congregation of Saints to acknowledge the Presidency as Prophets and Seers . . . to acknowledge the Twelve Apostles who were present as Prophets, Seers, Revelators, and special witnesses."

On January 19, 1841, Joseph and the assistant president and patriarch Hyrum Smith were both appointed by revelation as "a prophet, and a seer, and a revelator." (D&C 124:94.)

CHURCH ORGANIZED

On April 6, 1830, more than 30 people met at the home of Peter Whitmer Sr. to organize the Church of Jesus Christ. Some of them had already been baptized. Six were officially listed as organizers: Joseph Smith, Oliver Cowdery, Hyrum Smith, Peter Whitmer Jr., David Whitmer, and Samuel H. Smith.

Joseph was sustained first elder and Oliver Cowdery second elder. Joseph was also given the titles of seer, translator, and prophet. The sacrament was passed, and all present were individually confirmed and blessed with the gift of the Holy Ghost.

CHURCH NAMES

Although the Church was always understood to be Christ's restored church, its official name was changed several times early in this dispensation. When the Church was organized on April 6, 1830, it was referred to as the "Church of Christ." Then in the May 1834 conference held in Kirtland, members accepted the name "The Church of the Latter-day Saints." On April 26, 1838, in a revelation (D&C 115), the name was changed a final time to "The Church of Jesus Christ of Latter-day Saints." As early as August 1831 the term *Saints* was used in a revelation. Early nonmembers frequently referred to followers of Joseph Smith as "Mormons" and "Mormonites."

MENTOR-KIRTLAND CONVERTS

Four elders were called in September and October 1830 to teach the gospel to the Indians. The four, Peter Whitmer Jr., Parley P. Pratt, Ziba Peterson, and Oliver Cowdery, were to take their message to the Indian territory west of Missouri. However, their most important accomplishment may have been the baptism of 130 non-Indian converts in the Mentor-Kirtland area of northeast Ohio. Among this 130 were Sidney Rigdon, Frederick G. Williams, Newel K. Whitney, Lyman Wight, John Murdock, and Levi Hancock.

KIRTLAND

Kirtland Gathering

Kirtland was originally settled in 1818. Church members began gathering to Kirtland as early as 1831. This was the first in a succession of gathering places for the Saints. Nearly half of Joseph Smith's Doctrine and Covenants revelations were received in the Kirtland area. Here the Prophet worked on the inspired version of the Bible, created the first high council, organized Zion's Camp, established the School of the Prophets, and conducted the building of the first temple of this dispensation. Kirtland's LDS population grew from 100 in 1832 to more than 1,500 in 1836. By 1837 there were more Mormons than non-Mormons in Kirtland.

NEWELL K. WHITNEY (1795–1850)

Newell K. Whitney became one of Joseph Smith's trusted friends after they met during Joseph's first visit to Kirtland on February 1, 1831. Whitney was a successful merchant who had been baptized in November 1830. Joseph and Emma lived in the Whitney home for several weeks. In Whitney's store the Prophet received several revelations, including the Word of Wisdom and revelations on the priesthood (D&C 84 and 88) and the United Order. Work on the Bible translation and sessions of the School of the Prophets were also hosted in Whitney's store.

Newel Whitney was called as first bishop of Kirtland (December 4, 1831) and as presiding bishop (April 6, 1847). He died in Salt Lake City on September 23, 1850.

Pearl of Great Price

In July 1835 traveling promoter Michael Chandler brought an exhibit of four Egyptian mummies and papyri to Kirtland. Within days they were purchased by Church members and given to Joseph Smith, who immediately began to translate the ancient writings. He soon discovered they contained the writings of patriarchs Abraham and Joseph of Egypt. The book of Abraham, first published in the *Times and Seasons* in 1842, was published as part of the Pearl of Great Price in 1851. The Pearl of Great Price, accepted as scripture in 1880, consists of various sacred documents.

THE INSPIRED VERSION OF THE BIBLE

Commanded by God, Joseph Smith worked on an inspired translation of the Bible from June 1830 until July 1833. He was assisted first by Oliver Cowdery, then John Whitmer, and finally Sidney Rigdon. The translation consists of additions, deletions, and rearrangements—3,410 verses differ from the King James Bible. During Joseph's lifetime portions of this work were published in Church newspapers. In 1867 the Reorganized Church of Jesus Christ of Latter Day Saints, who own the original manuscript, published an edition of this Bible.

SCHOOL OF THE PROPHETS

The School of the Prophets was started by Joseph Smith in 1833 to prepare prospective missionaries in temporal and spiritual matters. The first school met in Kirtland on January 23, 1833, and ended in April 1833. In it, Joseph presided over the instruction of selected officers of the Church. The school was held periodically in Nauvoo and later in Utah.

FREDERICK G. WILLIAMS (1787–1842)

Born at Suffield, Connecticut, on October 28, 1787, Frederick G. Williams was one of the first high priests of the Church and the second counselor in the initial First Presidency (1833). Before joining the Church in October 1830, he was a prosperous and respected physician in the Kirtland area.

A close friend to Joseph Smith, Williams played an active role in building the Kirtland Temple, helped select the revelations to be included in the 1835 Doctrine and Covenants, served several short missions, was a member of Zion's Camp, and taught at the School of the Prophets.

He was rejected as second counselor in November 1837 and excommunicated in March 1839. He was restored to fellowship a year later on April 8, 1840. He died October 25, 1842, in Quincy, Illinois.

DOCTRINE AND COVENANTS

The Doctrine and Covenants, one of the Church's Standard Works, "is a collection of divine revelations and inspired declarations given for the establishment and regulation" of the Church. Most of the revelations were received by Joseph Smith, but others came through his successors. The earliest version of the Doctrine and Covenants was the Book of Commandments. In 1833 a Missouri mob destroyed the Church's printing press. Only 100 copies of the Book of Commandments containing 65 revelations were ever salvaged. In 1835 these revelations were included in a larger collection called the Doctrine and Covenants of the Church of Latter Day Saints, which contained 103 revelations or sections.

MISSOURI ZION

ZION

The Book of Mormon revealed that America would be the site of a New Jerusalem, the city of Zion, a place of gathering. In June 1831 Joseph Smith was directed to go to Missouri, where the location of Zion would be revealed.

After Joseph's arrival in Missouri, the Lord revealed, on July 20, 1831, that "the place which is now called Independence is the center; and a spot for the temple is lying westward, upon a lot which is not far from the court-house." (D&C 57.) On August 2, in a simple service, Sidney Rigdon dedicated and consecrated the land of Zion. The next day, Joseph dedicated the temple site.

The Saints, hoping for a permanent residence, bought land and built homes. After a year of peace, non-Mormon neighbors became hostile toward the Mormons. In 1833 the Saints were forced into neighboring Clay County.

ZION'S CAMP

In May and June of 1834, an expedition known as Zion's Camp set out from Kirtland to help the persecuted Saints 900 miles away in Clay County, Missouri. When Jackson County mobs learned of the well-armed Kirtland Saints, they burned the homes of the Mormons. The men of Zion's Camp quarreled with each other. Joseph Smith warned them that such conduct would bring a scourge upon the camp. On June 23, cholera struck the expedition at Clay County. Although Zion's Camp failed to stop the Missouri persecutions, the Church learned valuable lessons in organization, and nine of the first apostles were called from its ranks.

EDWARD PARTRIDGE (1793–1840)

Edward Partridge was the first bishop of the Church (1831). Born on August 27, 1793, in Pittsfield, Massachusetts, this prosperous hatter at first rejected the missionaries before being baptized by Joseph Smith in December 1830. On July 20, 1833, he was tarred and feathered by a Missouri mob demanding that Mormons leave Jackson County. He died in Nauvoo on May 27, 1840.

ADAM-ONDI-AHMAN

After being forced out of Jackson and Clay counties in Missouri, the Saints began settling in Caldwell and Daviess counties. In May 1838 Joseph Smith visited a site on the Grand River in Daviess county and declared it a new community, naming it Adam-ondi-Ahman. He explained that after Adam and Eve's expulsion from the Garden of Eden (located in Jackson County), they went to Adam-ondi-Ahman. There Adam blessed his family three years before his death. Joseph also said it is the place where Adam will visit his people.

WILLIAM WINES PHELPS (1792–1872)

Baptized on June 16, 1831, William W. Phelps was made editor of *The Evening and the Morning Star* in Independence, Missouri. He also served as first counselor in the first stake in Zion (Independence), scribe to Joseph Smith in the translation of the book of Abraham, and a member of Zion's Camp. Phelps was a gifted poet who wrote "The Spirit of God" and "Praise to the Man" along with thirteen other works found in today's hymnal. Excommunicated in 1839, he was readmitted in 1841. He died in Salt Lake City on March 6, 1872.

TWELVE APOSTLES

On February 14, 1835, the Three Witnesses chose the first Twelve Apostles in this dispensation:

Thomas B. Marsh	Parley P. Pratt	David W. Patten	Luke S. Johnson
Brigham Young	William Smith	Heber C. Kimball	Orson Pratt
Orson Hyde	John F. Boynton	William E. McLellin	Lyman E. Johnson

THOMAS B. MARSH (1799–1866)

First president of the Quorum of Twelve, Thomas R. Marsh was baptized by David Whitmer in September 1830. In 1837 Marsh worked to reconcile some of the Kirtland brethren who had "come out opposed to the Prophet." On February 10, 1838, Marsh was called as acting president of the Church in Missouri, replacing David Whitmer, who had fallen away. However, in August 1838, Marsh and his wife quarreled with other Saints over a trivial matter and soon became alienated from the Church. He was excommunicated on March 17, 1839. He rejoined the Church in July 1857 and died in Ogden, Utah, in January 1866.

KIRTLAND TEMPLE

Construction on the first temple of this dispensation began in June 1833. The Saints contributed a minimum of one day a week to the building of their temple.

On March 27, 1836, Joseph Smith dedicated the temple, noting in his dedicatory prayer, "Thou knowest that we have done this work through great tribulation; and out of poverty we have given of our substance to build a house to thy name, that the Son of Man might have a place to manifest himself to his people." (D&C 109:5.) People attending the dedication reported seeing angels and other heavenly manifestations.

The temple is 79 feet long, 59 feet wide, and 50 feet high (with the tower 110 feet high). It still stands; today it is owned by the Reorganized Church of Jesus Christ of Latter Day Saints.

PERSECUTION

EXODUS FROM OHIO

No official decision was made to leave Kirtland, but by early 1838 apostasy, financial failures, and anti-Mormon persecution spurred the LDS exodus from Kirtland and vicinity. Their lives threatened, Joseph Smith, Sidney Rigdon, and other leaders fled to Missouri in January 1838. In small groups of 50 or less, the Saints followed. A large group of 500 members in 59 wagons left Kirtland on July 5—the Kirtland Camp. By mid-summer, 1,600 Saints had left the Kirtland area; a few remained until they moved West in the 1840s.

DAVID W. PATTEN (1799–1838)

David W. Patten was baptized on June 15, 1832, and chosen as one of the original Twelve Apostles in February 1835. In early 1838, along with Thomas Marsh, he was called to be acting president of the Church in Missouri. Patten died October 25, 1838, from a bullet wound received from hostile Missourians at the battle of Crooked River—the Church's first martyr.

LILBURN BOGGS (1796–1860)

As governor of Missouri from 1836 to 1842, Lilburn Boggs came down squarely on the side of lawless Missouri mobocrats who were trying to kick the Mormons out of the state. Choosing to believe inflamed anti-Mormon reports, Boggs refused to listen to the Mormons' side. On October 27, 1838, he issued the cold-hearted "Extermination Order," which said, "The Mormons must be treated as enemies, and must be exterminated or driven from the state, if necessary, for the public good." Boggs later settled in California and died in 1860.

HAUN'S MILL MASSACRE

Missouri was filled with rumors that the Mormons were there to plunder and steal land from non-Mormons. By the fall of 1838, open conflicts grew in number and seriousness. Three days after the "Extermination Order," during a truce, 200 men of the Missouri militia made a surprise attack on the 30 families living at Jacob Haun's mill in Caldwell County. The attack was unprovoked and brutal. Women and children scattered into the woods while the men tried to defend the village from inside a log shop. Their makeshift fort became a trap when the militia shot through the spaces between the logs. In all, 17 Saints (including a 10-year-old boy) and one friendly non-Mormon were murdered; 13 were wounded. The panicked survivors dumped the dead bodies into a well before fleeing to safety.

PERSECUTION

ALEXANDER DONIPHAN (1808–1887)

On October 31, 1838, Joseph Smith, Sidney Rigdon, Parley P. Pratt, Lyman Wight, and George W. Robinson were arrested as they tried to negotiate peace with the mob. The next day Hyrum Smith and Amasa Lyman were arrested and, along with the others, sentenced by a secret court to die by firing squad. General Alexander Doniphan courageously refused to carry out the rder, writing to his superiors, "It is cold-blooded murder. I will not obey our order. . . . If you execute these men, I will hold you responsible before n earthly tribunal, so help me God." Doniphan would later serve with disnction in the Mexican and Civil Wars.

LIBERTY JAIL

Liberty Jail is a strange name for the prison in which Joseph and Hyrum Smith, Sidney Rigdon, Lyman Wight, Alexander McRae, and Caleb Baldwin were jailed for four months beginning December 1, 1838, on charges of treason. Conditions in the dimly lit dungeon were dirty and cold, with straw on the floor for beds and "coarse and filthy food." The revelations in D&C sections 121–23 are from a long letter of anguish and concern for the Saints that Joseph wrote from the jail on March 20–25, 1839. In April he and the others were allowed to "escape." (Rigdon, his health frail, had been released on bail in February.)

LYMAN WIGHT (1796–1858)

A veteran of the War of 1812, Lyman Wight was baptized by Oliver Cowdery in 1830. In 1831 Wight moved to Missouri, where, during the 1833 and 1838 persecutions, he led men to protect the Saints. He was also a member of Zion's Camp, after which he was ordained to the Missouri high council. He was an apostle from 1841 until excommunicated in 1848 for rejecting the leadership of Brigham Young and he Twelve. When the Church moved West, Wight moved to Texas to form splinter group. He died March 31, 1858.

EXODUS FROM MISSOURI

Having lost their homes and with their prophet jailed, more than ten thousand scattered Saints left Missouri under the direction of Brigham Young during the winter of 1838–1839. The Saints looked to Illinois for refuge. The citizens of Quincy, Illinois, compassionately aided the destitute Mormons. By April 22, 1839, Joseph and Hyrum Smith were able to join the Saints who had gathered in Illinois.

NAUVOO

After Joseph Smith arrived in Illinois, he chose the village Commerce as the place to regather the Saints. He changed the name to *Nauvoo,* from the Hebrew word for "beautiful." It would be the headquarters of the Church from 1839 to 1846. The Saints transformed the area from "literally a wilderness . . . covered with trees and bushes" into a thriving, vibrant "place of safety and gathering" that grew to nearly 12,000 inhabitants, rivaling the fast-growing Chicago.

In Nauvoo the Prophet wrote the Articles of Faith, published the book of Abraham, explained the origins and eternal destiny of mankind, established the Relief Society, introduced baptism for the dead and eternal marriage and began building the Nauvoo Temple.

JOHN C. BENNETT (1804–1867)

Baptized in September 1840, John C. Bennett, an energetic and talented doctor, served as mayor of Nauvoo, chancellor of the Nauvoo University, and major-general of the Nauvoo Legion. Most important to the Saints, Bennett was able to secure passage of the Nauvoo Charter in the Illinois General Assembly (December 16, 1840), which was actually three charters in one, granting Nauvoo city status, a university, and a city militia (the Nauvoo Legion).

On April 8, 1841, Joseph Smith called Bennett as assistant president in the First Presidency. Sexual misconduct led to Bennett's disfellowshipment on May 25, 1842, and his excommunication later that year. He published his hateful *The History of the Saints; or, An Exposé of Joe Smith and Mormonism.* Bennett died in Polk City, Iowa, in 1867.

ORRIN PORTER ROCKWELL (1813–1878)

Joseph Smith's bodyguard, and known as "The Destroying Angel," Orrin Porter Rockwell was baptized shortly after the organization of the Church. In 1842 he was arrested and charged with the attempted murder of Missouri governor Lilburn Boggs but was eventually released. Joseph gave Rockwell this promise, based on his faithfulness: "[If thou] cut not thy hair . . . no bullet or blade can harm thee." He did not cut his hair until 1855, when he did so to make a wig for an elderly Church member. In the Salt Lake Valley he was variously a rancher, lawman, Indian fighter, scout, and hotel keeper.

DROP IT!

EMMA HALE SMITH (1804–1879)

Emma Hale was born July 10, 1804, in Harmony, Pennsylvania, to Isaac and Elizabeth Hale. She met Joseph Smith in October 1825 when he was working for Josiah Stoal and boarding at her father's house. They eloped on January 18, 1827, and eventually became the parents of eleven children, five of whom reached adulthood: adopted daughter Julia, Joseph III, Frederick Granger Williams, Alexander Hale, and David Hyrum.

She helped Joseph with the Book of Mormon translation, was called to select hymns for the first hymnal, and was the first president of the Relief Society. As the wife of a man greatly loved and hated, she rarely knew a time free from anxiety and insecurity.

After Joseph's martyrdom, Emma married Lewis Bidamon on December 3, 1847. They lived in Nauvoo, where she died April 30, 1879. She is buried next to Joseph.

RELIEF SOCIETY

On the second floor of Joseph Smith's store in Nauvoo, on March 17, 1842, the Prophet "assisted in the organization" of the Female Relief Society, saying, "I now turn the key to you in the name of God and this Society shall rejoice and knowledge and intelligence shall flow down from this time." The 20 women present elected Emma Smith president, and she selected two counselors—Sarah Cleveland and Elizabeth Ann Whitney. The Relief Society helped in the construction of the temple, promoted moral reform, and donated to the poor.

By 1844 there were more than 1,300 members. The last Relief Society meeting recorded in Nauvoo was held on March 16, 1844. In 1867 President Brigham Young reorganized the Relief Society churchwide and called Eliza R. Snow as its president.

ELIZA R. SNOW (1804–1887)

Eliza R. Snow, "Zion's Poetess," was baptized in 1835. In Nauvoo she was the secretary of the Nauvoo Relief Society. On June 29, 1842, she was sealed as a plural wife to the Prophet. In 1867 Brigham Young called her to serve as president of the Relief Society. Over the next 20 years she helped found the *Woman's Exponent* with Louisa Greene, created the Primary Society at the recommendation of Aurelia Rogers, installed the Young Ladies' Retrenchment Association (Young Women), and was president of the board of directors of the Deseret Hospital Association.

LAMANITES

As early as 1830, Joseph Smith sent missionaries to various Native American tribes. In July 1836 the Saints were denounced, as the later were in Utah, for "declaring, even from the pulpit, that the Indians are a part of God's chosen people." On May 23, 1844, Joseph met members of the Sauk and Fox tribes, telling them "The Great Spirit has enabled me to find a book [showing them the Book of Mormon], which told me about your fathers

DEDICATION OF PALESTINE

Elder Orson Hyde climbed the Mount of Olives on October 24, 1841, to dedicate Palestine for the return of the Jews. It was the realization of a prophecy by the Prophet and Hyde's own 1840 vision. Hyde dedicated and consecrated the land "for the gathering together of Judah's scattered remnants." Fifty-six years later Jewish leaders met in a World Zionist Congress in Switzerland and called for the creation of a Jewish state in Palestine.

ORSON HYDE (1805–1878)

Baptized on October 30, 1831, by Sidney Rigdon, Orson Hyde was one of the original Twelve Apostles in this dispensation. He taught grammar in Kirtland, was a member of Zion's Camp, and was one of the first group of missionaries to England in 1837. In 1838 he was dropped from the Twelve for "failure to support the Church" but was resustained later the same year. In Utah he was called to head the Carson Valley Mission in 1855 and supervised settlement of the Sanpete area of Utah in 1858. He died in Spring City, Utah, in 1878.

NAUVOO LEGION

In 1840 the Nauvoo Legion was formed to protect the citizens of Nauvoo from mob violence. At its peak, the Legion was the largest Illinois militia with 5,000 men. Joseph Smith, as a lieutenant general, was commander of the Nauvoo Legion.

THE MISSION

BRITISH MISSION

Obeying Jesus' command to take the gospel "into all the world," Joseph Smith called Elders Heber C. Kimball and Orson Hyde to a mission in England. Joined by Willard Richards and Joseph Fielding, they departed Kirtland on June 13, 1837, and, with three additional missionaries, reached Liverpool July 20, 1837. Nine people were baptized on July 30, 1837. A foot race determined that George D. Watt would be the first convert baptized in England. Fifteen hundred people were converted by the time the missionaries returned home less than a year later in April 1838.

In early 1840 nine members of the Twelve arrived in Great Britain. In 15 months of proselyting, they converted 4,000; distributed 5,000 copies of the Book of Mormon, 3,000 hymnals, and 50,000 tracts; and helped 1,000 immigrants come to Nauvoo.

PARLEY P. PRATT (1807–1857)

Missionary, pamphleteer, and poet, Parley P. Pratt was baptized on September 1, 1830; he baptized his brother Orson two and a half weeks later on September 19. A month after that, Parley was called to preach to the Lamanites. He was ordained an apostle in February 1835; wrote the first missionary tract, *A Voice of Warning,* in 1837; proselyted in Canada; served a mission in England; and visited Chile in 1851. He was murdered on May 13, 1857, near Van Buren, Arkansas, while serving a mission.

WILLARD RICHARDS (1804–1854)

A fourth cousin to Joseph Smith, Dr. Willard Richards was baptized on December 31, 1836, by his first cousin Brigham Young. He was in the first group of missionaries to England in 1837. Ordained an apostle April 14, 1840, he was a secretary to Joseph and was with him at the martyrdom. He was sustained as second counselor to Brigham Young on December 27, 1847. He died in Salt Lake City on March 11, 1854.

GATHERING

A revelation given in September 1830 (D&C 29) told the Saints to gather to one place.

The two missions to Great Britain kindled the massive immigration of Saints from England (and later Europe) to Nauvoo and Utah. Immigration was the principal contributor to U.S. Church growth in the nineteenth century, providing leaders, educators, craftsmen, and artists. About 5,000 LDS British converts migrated to Nauvoo, and nearly 103,000 converts gathered to Zion between 1840 and 1910. Today, members all over the world are encouraged to build Zion in their own communities.

DEATH OF THE PROPHET

WILLIAM LAW (1809–1892)

Baptized in Canada in 1836, William Law moved to Nauvoo in late 1839. This wealthy businessman became a Nauvoo city councilman and was named second counselor to Joseph Smith on January 19, 1841. He was also one of the first to receive the endowment. He broke with the Church over polygamy and was excommunicated on April 18, 1844. After his excommunication Law openly opposed Joseph and helped publish the anti-Mormon *Nauvoo Expositor*. Law died in Wisconsin on January 19, 1892.

NAUVOO EXPOSITOR

In the spring of 1844 anti-Mormons, excommunicated members, and unhappy members worked together to bring down Joseph Smith. They claimed he was a fallen prophet for teaching polygamy, but they also feared his political power as mayor, commander of the Nauvoo Legion, and justice of the peace. To undermine the Prophet, they published the inflammatory *Nauvoo Expositor*.

On June 10, 1844, at the Prophet's urging, the Nauvoo city council declared the newspaper a "public nuisance." The destruction of the press incited the Prophet's enemies and led to his arrest for treason.

MARTYRDOM

Following the destruction of the *Nauvoo Expositor*, Governor Thomas Ford ordered Joseph Smith to stand trial for treason. On June 23, 1844, Joseph and Hyrum crossed the Mississippi River to seek refuge in the West. The pleas of family and friends brought them back, though Joseph prophesied, "I am going like a lamb to the slaughter." Governor Ford promised their safety and sent them to Carthage Jail.

Late on the afternoon of June 27, a mob of 200 men gathered. They muddied their faces, stormed into the jail, charged up the stairs, and fired through the door into the room that held Joseph, Hyrum, John Taylor, and Willard Richards. Shot in the face, Hyrum fell, saying, "I am a dead man!" Joseph shot into the crowded hall. With muskets and bayonets filling the doorway, Taylor tried to escape out a window but was shot five times. He then rolled under the bed. Richards was not wounded.

At an open window, Joseph was struck in the collarbone and the chest. Fatally wounded, he fell out the window—his last words were "Oh Lord, my God!"

AFTER JOSEPH

SUCCESSION

The murder of the Prophet created a crisis—who would lead the Church after Joseph Smith? Except for John Taylor and Willard Richards, the Twelve were away on missions but returned to Nauvoo quickly upon learning of the Prophet's death. On August 6 Brigham Young arrived to find Sidney Rigdon claiming that he (Rigdon), as counselor to Joseph Smith, should be the Church's next leader.

On August 8, 1844, members gathered "to choose a guardian, or President and Trustee." Rigdon spoke first, and then Young, who stated in part, "Without a Prophet at our head, do I step forth to act in my calling in connection with the Quorum of Twelve . . . who are ordained and anointed to bear off the keys of the kingdom of God in all the world."

The members overwhelmingly chose Brigham and the Twelve to lead the Church.

SIDNEY RIGDON (1793–1876)

Baptized in November 1830, Sidney Rigdon was one of Joseph Smith's closest advisors and was first counselor in the First Presidency from 1833 to 1844. He helped Joseph with the translation of the Bible, was with him during nine revelations, and worked with him on the Book of Moses. Along with Joseph he was tarred and feathered and also imprisoned in Liberty Jail. In Nauvoo, Rigdon served as city attorney. When Joseph ran for the U.S. presidency in 1844, Rigdon was his running mate. After the martyrdom, when Rigdon's claim to Church leadership was rejected, he refused to follow Brigham and the Twelve. Excommunicated in September 1844, he moved to Pennsylvania and organized a Church of Christ. He died in Friendship, New York.

NAUVOO TEMPLE

Construction of the Nauvoo Temple began in March 1841. It occupied much of the Saints' emotional, spiritual, and physical energies until they left the city in 1846. As sections of the temple were completed, they were dedicated and used. To avoid potential mob action (anti-Mormons were attempting to destroy the temple), a private dedication took place on April 30, 1846, followed by a public dedication on May 1–3, 1846.

The temple was made of light gray limestone and had sixty rooms. It was 128 feet long, 88 feet wide, and 65 feet high, with a tower and spire reaching 165 feet. It was destroyed by arson fire and tornado. One of the sunstones from the temple has been on display in the Smithsonian Institution in Washington, D.C.

THE TREK WEST

BRIGHAM YOUNG (1801–1877)

BRIGHAM YOUNG ABOUT 1850

Lion of the Lord, American Moses, and second president of the Church, Brigham Young was the ninth of 11 children born to John and Abigail Young. He grew up on a farm learning to plant, cultivate, and harvest. During his teens he was an apprentice carpenter, painter, and glazier. Baptized in June 1832, he was ordained an apostle in February 1835. In the winter of 1838–1839, he directed the Saints' exodus from Missouri. Brigham was a missionary to England in early 1840. In Nauvoo he coordinated missionary work, construction projects, and the settling of immigrants. He was among those taught the doctrine of plural marriage. He was also among the first to receive the temple endowment from Joseph Smith. At the time of Joseph's murder he was in Boston. Arriving in Nauvoo in August, he and the Twelve were sustained to lead the Church.

PIONEERS

Anti-Mormon feelings grew so strong in Nauvoo that Brigham Young decided to move the Saints West. On a cold February 1846 night, Saints crossed the frozen Mississippi River to begin the trek West. A steady stream left the Nauvoo area throughout the winter and spring of 1846, and by fall the city was almost deserted. As the Saints moved across Iowa, they established numerous settlements. In fact, until the fall of 1848, Winter Quarters, then Kanesville (Council Bluffs), was Church headquarters. At one point, it had an LDS population of 8,000. In 1852 the majority of the Saints remaining in Iowa left for the Salt Lake Valley.

The pioneers traveled in wooden wagons that were 4 feet wide, 10 feet long, and topped with canvas waterproofed with linseed oil. The wagons could carry up to 2,000 pounds and were pulled by ox teams.

Between 1847 and 1869 wagon trains and handcart companies moved more than 70,000 Saints West. The Mormons were part of a great nineteenth-century venture in which more than 300,000 people moved West on the Mormon, Oregon, and California trails.

PERPETUAL EMIGRATION FUND

Since most converts lacked enough money to emigrate, the Church organized a fund, in 1849, to which people could donate and provide emigrants with a loan. The repayments then helped other travelers. From 1850 to 1887 the fund helped 26,000 LDS emigrants.

999,999 bottles of root beer on the wall... Take one down, Pass it around; 999,999 bottles of root beer... 999,998...

THEY REALLY DID SING AS THEY WALKED AND WALKED AND WALKED ON

THE TREK WEST

WILLIAM CLAYTON (1814–1879)

Born July 17, 1814, in Penwortham, England, William Clayton was baptized in the River Ribble by Heber C. Kimball. After arriving in Nauvoo in December 1840, he was private secretary to Joseph Smith, recorder of the temple, and city treasurer. He was present when Joseph received the revelation on celestial marriage. On April 15, 1846, in honor of his son's birth, he wrote the stirring hymn "Come, Come Ye Saints." In Utah he cut the dies for the "Mormon money" (p. 24), was secretary to the territorial legislature, and was a shopkeeper and a farmer. He died in Salt Lake City on December 4, 1879.

MORMON BATTALION

While the Saints were encamped in Iowa, the United States persuaded Church leaders to provide men to serve in the Mexican War. In return, the "Mormon soldiers" would receive pay, clothing, and rations. On July 16, 1846, at Council Bluffs, Iowa, 543 men joined the Mormon Battalion. Four days later, with 33 women and 51 children, they left Iowa for a 2,000-mile march to California through Kansas, New Mexico, and Arizona. They were released from duty on July 16, 1847, in Los Angeles. Fortunately, they never fought a battle.

HANDCART PIONEERS

Because it was expensive to outfit a full wagon and ox team, Brigham Young suggested the use of handcarts as an inexpensive way for poor Saints to travel overland to Utah.

Modeled after street-sweepers' carts, the wooden, two-wheeled handcarts were as wide as a wagon and six feet long; the carrying box was three to four feet long and eight inches high. The carts could carry up to 500 pounds. Usually two people took turns pulling and pushing.

The handcart companies were begun in 1856. The first three companies safely made the 1,300-mile trip from Iowa City to Salt Lake City. However, the two late-starting Willie and Martin companies were caught in late fall blizzards, in which 213 of 980 immigrants died. Brigham Young organized a successful massive relief effort.

After 1856, five more companies made the trip West, the last company in 1860. In all, 2,962 immigrants pulled handcarts to Utah with 250 deaths.

THIS IS THE PLACE

BROOKLYN SAINTS

When the Mormons fled Nauvoo, Saints in the eastern states joined the exodus west. On February 4, 1846, 238 Mormons, led by Samuel Brannan, boarded the ship *Brooklyn* and sailed from New York harbor on a 17,000-mile journey to California around Cape Horn. During the voyage, there were 12 deaths and two births—one baby was named Atlantic and the other Pacific. They arrived in San Francisco on July 31. While some stayed in California, including Sam Brannan, others eventually moved to Utah.

SAMUEL BRANNAN (1819–1889)

After his baptism in 1833, Samuel Brannan served as a missionary and presided over the Eastern Saints. In 1846 Brigham Young had him organize the voyage of the *Brooklyn*.

After leading the *Brooklyn* Saints to San Francisco, Brannan tried to get President Young to move the Saints to California. He remained in California, where he made a fortune during the gold rush. He was excommunicated for "unchristianlike" conduct on September 1, 1851. He died penniless on May 6, 1889, in Escondido, California.

The first company of 143 men, 3 women, 2 children, 17 dogs, 52 mules, 66 oxen, 93 horses, and 72 wagons left Winter Quarters on April 5, 1847. After traveling 1,032 miles, they arrived at the Valley of the Great Salt Lake on July 24, 1847, with Brigham Young declaring, "This is the right place, drive on." Two other companies arrived before winter.

THIS IS THE PLACE

ORSON PRATT (1811–1881)

One of the original Twelve, Orson Pratt was a missionary, editor, writer, mathematician, and pioneer. He was a member of Zion's Camp, missionary to England, and leader of the European Mission. Excommunicated in August 1842 over polygamy, he was reinstated into the Quorum of the Twelve in January 1843.

He and Erastus Snow were the first Saints to enter the Salt Lake Valley, on July 21, 1847—three days before the main body of Saints. Brigham Young assigned him to publicly announce the doctrine of plural marriage at a conference held in August 1852. He died on October 3, 1881.

HOME IN THE WILDERNESS

FIRST SETTLEMENT

Upon their arrival in the Salt Lake Valley, the pioneers planted late crops, built temporary shelters, laid out streets, and chose the temple site. On August 9, 1847, Young Elizabeth Steele became the first white child born in Utah. In August Brigham Young and others left to return to Winter Quarters to prepare the remaining Saints for the 1848 trek.

Before winter the pioneers built a walled fort near today's Pioneer Park. They constructed 450 log cabins, cultivated 5,133 acres, and planted 872 acres of winter wheat. During that first winter, 1,650 pioneers stayed in the Salt Lake Valley.

MARY FIELDING SMITH (1801–1852)

A pioneer of faith and courage, Mary Fielding Smith was the wife of Hyrum Smith, mother of LDS Church president Joseph F. Smith, and grandmother of President Joseph Fielding Smith. After leaving Nauvoo in the fall of 1846, she and her children spent 18 months at Winter Quarters before crossing the plains in 1848. Nine-year-old Joseph F. drove a wagon. She farmed in the Mill Creek area of the Salt Lake Valley until her death on September 21, 1852 (probably from pneumonia).

HEBER C. KIMBALL (1810–1868)

Heber C. Kimball was a missionary, one of the original apostles, pioneer, first counselor to President Brigham Young, and grandfather of President Spencer W. Kimball. He led six others on the first mission to England in 1837. While Joseph Smith was imprisoned in Liberty Jail, he helped Brigham organize the Saints fleeing Missouri. He was first counselor in the First Presidency from December 5, 1847, until his death on June 22, 1868, from injuries sustained in a carriage accident.

CRICKETS AND GULLS

In the spring of 1848 the Salt Lake Saints planted new crops. A drought hit in May and June. Then swarms of crickets, which the pioneers said looked like a cross between a spider and a buffalo, began devouring the crops. For two weeks everyone battled the crickets with sticks, brooms, and shovels. They tried burning and even drowning them. Defeated and exhausted, the Saints prayed. From the Great Salt Lake, seagulls flew in and for weeks gorged on crickets.

These "crickets" were actually large, wingless grasshoppers that the Indians taught the Mormons to mash, roast, and bake into their bread.

HEY! THIS RAISIN BREAD IS GREAT!

THOSE AREN'T RAISINS.

DESERET

STATE OF DESERET

In 1849 Brigham Young outlined the borders for the State of Deseret—an area of 490,000 square miles (Utah is 82,168).

Deseret is a Book of Mormon word meaning "honeybee." Deseret was dissolved on March 28, 1851, after the smaller Utah Territory, with Brigham as governor, was created by the United States.

MORMON MONEY

The first "money" used in pioneer Utah was California gold dust weighed, wrapped in paper, and signed by Brigham Young and Willard Richards. Gold coins were minted in 1849 and 1850. On one side was the motto "Holiness to the Lord" along with a three-pointed crown over an all-seeing eye; on the other side appeared the value, two clasped hands (symbolizing friendship), and the letters "G.S.L.C.P.G." (Great Salt Lake City Pure Gold).

Paper currency was also issued at different times. One kind of paper money, issued from 1857 to 1860, was backed by livestock and certified with Brigham Young's signature.

DESERET ALPHABET

Announced on April 8, 1852, the Deseret Alphabet was a new phonetic system of writing English. One of its goals was to help foreign converts learn to read English. It employed 38 characters corresponding to English sounds. First and secondary school readers were published in 1868; the Book of Mormon was published in 1869. It met with limited success and ended with the death of Brigham Young.

A .... Ɛ
B .... Ƀ
Z 6

BEEHIVE

Used by pioneer Saints on buildings, furniture, and goods (and on the current Utah State Seal), the beehive symbolizes industry and the "harmony, order and frugality of the people, and of the sweet result of their toil." This type of beehive (called a *skep*) dates back to the European Middle Ages and is made of straw reinforced with clay.

LIKE MY HAIR?

INDICANS

As the Mormons colonized the Great Basin, they encountered Indians. Although there were conflicts, Brigham Young instructed the Saints to be kind and to feed rather than fight the Indians. Mormon pioneers befriended and offered Church membership to Indians, inviting them to participate in every aspect of the gospel. Special missionary efforts were made throughout the Intermountain West. The year 1875 was the peak of Indian baptisms—George Washington Hill reported 808, and Dimick Huntington recorded another 2,000.

JACOB HAMBLIN (1819–1886)

Brigham Young called Jacob Hamblin the "apostle to the Lamanites," although he was never an apostle.

A longtime friend and missionary to the Paiute, Navajo, and Hopi Indians, Jacob was often asked to ease tensions between settlers and Indians, sometimes at great personal risk.

While living in Tooele in the early 1850s, he was about to kill an Indian but was divinely inspired: "If you do not shed the blood of an Indian, not one of them shall ever have power to shed yours." In 1854 he established the Indian Mission in southern Utah and later helped settle Santa Clara. He died at Pleasanton, New Mexico, in August 1886.

LITTLE SOLDIER (1821–1884)

A Gosiute Indian, Little Soldier was born in the foothills of present-day Salt Lake City. As leader of his band, he set a tone of peace and friendship with settlers. Little Soldier, his wife, and several of his band were baptized on June 6, 1874. The next year, at the Endowment House, he and his wife received their endowments and had their marriage sealed for eternity. Little Soldier was called "to preaching to the other Indians," and he worked with missionaries and Indians in farming efforts in Corrine and on the Bear River. He died near Ogden on April 22, 1884.

HOME INDUSTRY

To promote a self-reliant local economy free of non-Mormon influences (moral as well as economic), Brigham Young encouraged home industry based on exchange of goods and labor rather than money. Throughout the settlements, Saints were encouraged to grow, build, create, and manufacture. One enterprise included the importation of mulberry trees and silkworms to start a silk industry. The undertaking had limited success, but many of the mulberry trees still remain.

Other home industries included farming, ranching, and making clothing, paper, rope, toys, tools, beds, paper, brooms, wagons, jewelry, and farm machinery.

UTAH WAR

In response to one-sided reports that Mormons were in rebellion, i 1857 President James Buchanan sent 2,500 troops to impose U.S authority and replace Brigham Young as governor. When Colonel Albert S Johnston's troops reached central Wyoming, Mormon raiding partie burned their supply wagons and drove away their livestock. The army wa forced to winter about 130 miles east of Salt Lake City. The Eastern pres began to call the enterprise "Buchanan's Blunder."

Thomas L. Kane arrived in February 1858 to negotiate a peace. Fol lowing Brigham's orders 30,000 Mormons left their homes in Norther Utah. Plans were made to burn Salt Lake City to the ground if the army trie to occupy it. After negotiations, the Mormons accepted a new governo and on June 26 Johnston's army was allowed to travel through the empt Salt Lake City and set up camp 40 miles to the southwest.

DANIEL H. WELLS (1814–1891)

A non-Mormon Nauvoo resident, Daniel H. Wells served as a university trustee and a Nauvoo Legion general. Baptized on August 9, 1846, his wife, Eliza, refused to join the Church or go West. Commander of the Utah Nauvoo Legion and second counselor to Brigham Young (1857), he led Mormon guerrilla forces against Johnston's army. Elected in 1866, he served for 10 years as mayo of Salt Lake City. He died March 24, 1891. His son, Heber Wells, becam Utah's first state governor.

ALBERT S. JOHNSTON (1803–1862)

Albert S. Johnston graduated from West Point i 1826. In 1857 he was appointed to lead the Utal Expedition. During the Civil War he commande Confederate troops west of the Appalachian Moun tains. He was shot in the leg and bled to death at th Battle of Shiloh, in 1862.

THOMAS L. KANE (1822–1883)

Though a non-Mormon, Thomas L. Kane was a long-time friend of the Saints. He first became aware of them in 1846. In Washington, D.C., he used his con-tacts to solicit help for the migrating Mormons; his efforts created the mutually beneficial Mormon Battalion. While visiting the Mormons camped on the Missouri River, he contracted tuberculosis. Nursed to health by the Saints, he thereafte devoted himself to helping them. He negotiated a peace to the Utah War promoted Utah statehood, and gave pro-Mormon lectures in the East When Brigham Young died, Kane returned to Utah to express his sorrow and comfort his friends, the Mormons.

PROBLEMS AND PROGRESS

AMERICAN CIVIL WAR, 1861–1865

In 1832 Joseph Smith prophesied that the "Southern States shall be divided against the Northern States." (D&C 87:3.) In the first message sent on the Overland Telegraph in October 1861, Brigham Young assured the country, "Utah has not seceded, but is firm for the Constitution."

The U.S. army left Utah in 1861 but returned in October 1862 under the command of Col. Patrick Connor. To the Saints' chagrin, Connor established Ft. Douglas near Salt Lake City, promoted non-Mormon immigration, and encouraged mining. In 1863 he and his troops slaughtered 250 Shoshoni men, women, and children camped on the Bear River near Preston, Idaho.

Though the nation was torn by conflict, LDS immigration to Utah remained high during the Civil War—13,202 people from 1861 to 1865.

BLACK HAWK WAR

BLACK HAWK

Although the Saints practiced kindness toward Indians, skirmishes sometimes occurred. Beginning in the spring of 1865, a young Ute named Black Hawk led 200 warriors on a four-year campaign against settlers. The federal government refused to help; instead, the Utah Nauvoo Legion and volunteers defended southern Utah settlements. In 1869 Black Hawk and his forces walked into a Fillmore Sunday meeting and announced they "desired a lasting peace."

Cost to the Saints: 70 men killed, 2,000 head of livestock lost, and 25 settlements abandoned. Cost to the Indians: displacement and life on the reservation.

TABERNACLE

The building of the Tabernacle was announced in April 1863, and the cornerstones were laid July 26, 1864. Bridge builder Henry Grow headed the construction and designed a lattice of huge arched trusses. The trusses were constructed of timber held together with wooden pegs and, if cracked, bound with rawhide.

Known for its superb acoustics, the Tabernacle was completed and used in 1867 and the balcony added in 1869–1870. It was not dedicated until 1875. It holds 10,000 people.

BALLANTYNE SUNDAY SCHOOL

R. BALLANTYNE

On December 9, 1849, Scottish convert Richard Ballantyne taught the first LDS Sunday School as fifty children gathered in his Salt Lake home. Ballantyne felt it his calling to teach children "the goodness of God, and the true Gospel." Soon other Sunday Schools were organized in the valley. The Deseret Sunday School Union was organized in November 1867. Nearly 15,000 children and adults were attending 200 Sunday Schools by 1870.

GOLDEN SPIKE

The joining of the transcontinental railroad on May 10, 1869, a Promontory, Utah, brought an end to the Saints' isolation. It als ended the era of wagon trains; an Iowa-to-Utah wagon trek took three t four months, but a *transcontinental* railway trip took only eight days. Th railroad opened up the West. To counter non-Mormon influences, the Reli Society was reemphasized, the School of the Prophets reorganized, Sunda Schools revitalized, the Young Ladies' Retrenchment Association estab lished, and cooperatives set up.

ZCMI

The first Zion's Cooperative Mercantile Institution opened for business on March 1, 1869, in Salt Lake City. Part of an effort to intensify home industry and to boycott profiteering non-Mormon merchants, Brigham Young established ZCMI "to bring goods here and sell them as low as they can possibly be sold." The store gave prior ity to selling Mormon home industry goods. Eventually ZCMI had its own factories for men's underwear, shirts, vests, overalls, coats, shoes, and boots.

Within six weeks of the first store opening, 81 branch stores were in busi ness throughout the territory.

WILLIAM S. GODBE (1833–1902)

An English convert, William S. Godbe arrived in Uta in 1851. A wealthy merchant, he donated mor tha $50,000 to the Church and $200,000 to the arts. H served as counselor in the Thirteenth Ward bishopri and was a member of the School of the Prophets. I 1868 he bitterly objected to Brigham Young's politica and economic power and sided with non-Mormon business men. Excommunicated in 1869, he and other disenchanted Mormon became known as "Godbeites." The Godbeites created the *Mormo Tribune* (later the *Salt Lake Tribune*). He died August 1, 1902, at his sum mer cabin at Brighton, Utah.

COMING OF THE RAILROAD

REDEDICATION

RETRENCHMENT ASSOCIATIONS

The Young Ladies' Retrenchment Association and the Senior Cooperative Retrenchment Association were started in 1869 and 1870 by Brigham Young to help LDS women avoid worldliness, maintain Mormon uniqueness, and cultivate moral and mental development. To this end the Retrenchment Associations held semimonthly inspirational meetings, helped facilitate home industry, and publicly supported polygamy. A "retrenchment dress" that emphasized modesty and simplicity was also designed for young women.

The Young Ladies' Retrenchment Association, first organized among Brigham Young's daughters, later became the Young Ladies' Mutual Improvement Association.

MARY ISABELLA HORNE (1818–1905)

President of the Senior Cooperative Retrenchment Association from 1870 to 1904, Mary Isabella Horne accepted Brigham Young's 1869 challenge to inspire women to spend time perfecting their spirituality and becoming less materialistic.

She and her husband, Joseph Horne, were the parents of 15 children, including three sets of twins. She was also president of the Salt Lake Stake Relief Society for 26 years, a member of the Deseret Hospital board, and a counselor in the presidency of the Deseret Silk Association. She died August 25, 1905, in Salt Lake City.

UNITED ORDER

Initiated to minimize dependency on non-Mormons and to promote LDS unity, more than 200 United Orders were established throughout the Great Basin, Canada, and Mexico. The first United Order was organized in St. George on February 9, 1874, and the last one was founded in Chihuahua, Mexico, in January 1893. The "orders" varied in form and enterprise, but most were organized to pool property and capital so that members shared the net income of their enterprise rather than receiving wages. By the time of Brigham Young's death in 1877, most of the United Orders had failed. Some functioned into the 1890s and early 1900s.

ELLIS R. SHIPP (1847–1939)

Dr. Ellis R. Shipp was an 1878 graduate of the Woman's Medical College of Pennsylvania. She was a staff physician at Deseret Hospital, founder of a school of nursing, co-editor of a pioneer medical journal, and member of the Relief Society General Board. She helped deliver 5,000 babies during her 60-year medical career. In 1866 she married Dr. Milford B. Shipp, and they were the parents of 10 children; number 6 was born during her second year of studies.

EDUCATING THE SAINTS

BYU AND CHURCH EDUCATION

As non-Mormons moved into Utah Territory, there were conflicts over teaching Mormon values in the schools. The Saints did not want to lose control of educating their children. To emphasize this point, in October 1875 Brigham Young donated a building in Provo to establish Brigham Young Academy. The school opened in January 1876, and that April Karl G. Maeser was called to lead the academy with the challenge that "neither the alphabet nor the multiplication table were to be taught without the Spirit of God." From its first 67 students the academy grew into Brigham Young University, now with more than 27,000 students.

Between 1876 and 1910, 32 more local academies were established throughout the Great Basin, Canada, and Mexico. Because of financial burdens, the rise in public education, and the success of seminaries, all but three (BYU, Ricks College, and Juárez Academy) were closed or turned over to states by the mid-1930s.

KARL G. MAESER (1828–1901)

Born and educated in Germany, Karl G. Maeser was one of the pioneering educators of the Church. Baptized in 1855, he arrived in Utah in 1860. In 1861 he was in charge of Salt Lake Union Academy. Three years later he was a private tutor for the Brigham Young family. Multi-talented, he played the organ for the Tabernacle Choir, taught music, and spoke French, Latin, German, Italian, and English. In April 1876 he was appointed the principal of the newly founded Brigham Young Academy, and in 1888 he was called to be the first superintendent of all Church schools.

PRIMARY

In the summer of 1878 Aurelia Spencer Rogers talked to Eliza R. Snow about the need to teach children the gospel. Soon thereafter President John Taylor authorized the establishment of the Primary. On August 25, 1878, with Aurelia as president, 224 girls and boys met for the first Primary class. By the mid-1880s most LDS settlements had a Primary. In 1913, a Primary wing was established in Salt Lake City's Grove's Latter-day Saints Hospital. The Primary Children's Hospital opened in 1952.

AURELIA SPENCER ROGERS (1834–1922)

Her mother dead and her father on a mission in Europe, 13-year-old Aurelia Spencer guided her five brothers and sister across the plains in 1848. Her father, Orson Spencer, joined them in Salt Lake City a year later. Aurelia married Thomas Rogers in 1851, and they moved to Farmington, Utah.

As well as founding the Primary, Aurelia served on its general board, served 22 years as secretary of the Farmington Relief Society, was a delegate to the Women's Suffrage Convention and the National Council of Women, and raised 10 children.

DEATH OF BRIGHAM YOUNG

In his 30 years as Church president, Brigham Young moved the Saints from Nauvoo to Utah, organized the immigration of 70,000 converts, championed goodwill with Indians, established more than 350 communities, directed an increasingly successful missionary program, fostered numerous social and economic programs to keep the Saints self-reliant, initiated a Church education system, started the United Order, encouraged the founding of auxiliaries, saw to the building of four temples, and, in his last year, directed a major priesthood reorganization of stakes and defined the responsibilities of ward and stake leaders.

On August 23, 1877, after meeting with bishops in the Council House, Brigham Young became ill with cramps and vomiting. "The Lion of the Lord" died on August 29, at the age of 76, of peritonitis, the result of a ruptured appendix. His last words were "Joseph! Joseph! Joseph!"

SUCCESSION

Unlike Joseph Smith's death, Brigham Young's death left no doubt as to who should lead the Church—the duties of the First Presidency were now with the Quorum of the Twelve. It was clearly defined that the senior member of the Twelve was to be the next president of the Church, but the question was *when* the new First Presidency should be organized and set apart. John Taylor did not become president until 1880, three years after the death of Brigham Young. After President Taylor's death in 1887, Wilford Woodruff was made president in 1889. However, Wilford Woodruff instructed Lorenzo Snow that the First Presidency should be immediately organized after the death of a president. Eleven days after President Woodruff's death, Lorenzo Snow was named president of the Church. This example of organizing a First Presidency without delay has been followed ever since.

JOHN TAYLOR (1808–1887)

John Taylor, the third president of the Church, was born in Milnthorpe, England. He moved to Canada in 1832 and was baptized there in 1836. On December 19, 1838, Brigham Young ordained him an apostle. A gifted writer, he published *The Times and Seasons* and the *Nauvoo Neighbor*.

John Taylor was with Joseph and Hyrum Smith when they were martyred. Wounded by four musket balls, with another hitting his watch, he became known as the "living martyr." He authored the beautiful tribute to the fallen brothers in D&C 135.

JOHN TAYLOR ABOUT 1853

After Brigham Young's death, John Taylor led the Church as the senior apostle until he was set apart as president in October 1880. His motto signified his loyalty to the gospel: "The kingdom of God or nothing."

PLURAL MARRIAGE

POLYGAMY RUNDOWN:
JOSEPH SMITH TO EDMUNDS-TUCKER

Mormon polygamy allowed a man to marry more than one woman. After the July 1843 revelation on eternal marriage and the "plurality of wives" (D&C 132), the practice of polygamy remained a secret. On August 1852 the doctrine was made public by Orson Pratt in a special LDS conference.

This caused outrage among Americans, who considered polygamy immoral. Congress worked hard to outlaw the practice. The Republican Party pledged to end "the twin relics of barbarism—polygamy and slavery."

In 1862 the Morrill Act made "bigamy" a crime in territories; however few Mormons were tried under this law. In 1882 the Edmunds Act toughened anti-polygamy laws and intensified prosecution efforts. In 1887 Congress passed the Edmunds-Tucker Act, which called for the disenfranchisement of polygamists and allowed federal officials to confiscate Church property.

GEORGE REYNOLDS (1842–1909)

In 1874 the Church decided to have a "test case" brought before the Supreme Court to test the constitutionality of the Morrill Anti-bigamy Act. They chose 32-year-old English convert George Reynolds, who was Brigham Young's secretary and a husband of two wives. In March 1875 Reynolds was convicted and sentenced to two years in prison and fined $500. A year later the conviction was overturned by the Utah Supreme Court but was upheld in 1879 by the U.S. Supreme Court. After serving 18 months, Reynolds was released in January 1881. He was a secretary to the First Presidency until his death. In 1890 he was called as a president of the First Quorum of Seventy. He spent 21 years writing the two-volume *A Complete Concordance of the Book of Mormon*.

RUDGER CLAWSON (1857–1943)

On October 15, 1884, the first case was prosecuted under the Edmunds Act. Newly appointed Judge Charles S. Zane found 27-year-old Rudger Clawson guilty. Clawson received a particularly harsh sentence of four years in prison and a fine of $800. After serving three years, one month, and 10 days, Clawson was pardoned by President Grover Cleveland on December 12, 1887. Interestingly, his father, Hiram Clawson, joined him in prison in November 1885 but only for six months. Rudger Clawson was ordained an apostle on October 10, 1898.

SUGAR HOUSE PRISON

Between 1884 and 1893 nearly 1,000 Saints were sent to prison for polygamy. Most of the convicted spent 6 to 18 months in a run-down adobe prison on the site of present-day Sugar House Park in Salt Lake City.

Living conditions in the overcrowded prison were less than ideal. Rudger Clawson claimed that "a man could write his name with the blood of bugs by pressing his finger against them as they crawled along the wall over the frame work of the bunks." However, the imprisoned Saints made the best of a dreadful situation. John Jones joined a prisoner band and played for "grand marches" within the prison. "Thus," he wrote, "we made our prison life as happy as possible."

GEORGE Q. CANNON (1827–1901)

A member of the First Presidency since 1873, George Q. Cannon had been a missionary to Hawaii, translated the Book of Mormon into Hawaiian, and been elected a territorial delegate to Congress in 1872. After being arrested and then failing to appear for trial in 1886, he remained in hiding until September 1888, when he turned himself over to federal officials. He entered prison on September 17 and served until February 21, 1889. He used his prison time well by working on a biography of Joseph Smith, writing magazine articles, and organizing a prison Sunday School. He founded a publishing firm, George Q. Cannon and Sons, which later became Deseret Book Company.

CHURCH PROPERTY AND DISENFRANCHISEMENT

The Edmunds-Tucker Act of 1887 was created by Congress to keep polygamists from serving on juries, holding public office, and voting. Nearly 12,000 Utahns lost their right to vote. Idaho enacted a loyalty oath in 1885 that effectively banned all Mormons from voting.

The Edmunds Act of 1882 also authorized seizure of Church real estate in excess of $50,000, disbanded the Utah Nauvoo Legion, and dissolved the Perpetual Emigration Fund. The Church was able to turn some property over to trusted individuals. However, federal agents confiscated about $800,000 of property and then rented needed buildings back to the Church, including the Salt Lake Temple block.

AND IF YOU WANT TO SEE PICTURES OF MY KIDS I'LL HAVE TO GET MY OTHER 10 WALLETS.

TRANSITION

MARTHA HUGHES CANNON (1857–1932)

A polygamous wife of Angus M. Cannon, Dr. Martha Hughes Cannon earned a medical degree from the University of Michigan at age 23. In 1897 she defeated her husband to become the first female state senator in the United States. She was the mother of three, a faithful Mormon, and an independent thinker who worked for women's rights. Her ongoing concern for public health motivated Dr. Cannon to lead a successful effort to abolish the use of tin cups that were chained to public drinking fountains.

JOHN TAYLOR DIES IN HIDING

President John Taylor presided over troubled times for the Saints. He was able to hold the Church together during the increasingly harsh anti-polygamy/anti-Mormon campaign of the 1880s. In 1885 President Taylor and other Church leaders "went underground" (into hiding) to avoid arrest and harassment from federal marshals. Directing the Church by letters, President Taylor was able to create four new missions; establish LDS settlements in Colorado, Wyoming, and Arizona; oversee the founding of the Primary; and dedicate the Logan Temple. He died at the Thomas Roueche home in Kaysville, Utah, on July 25, 1887—a "double martyr" for his near-fatal wounds at Carthage and dying in exile.

WILFORD WOODRUFF (1807–1898)

Wilford Woodruff, the fourth president of the Church, was baptized on December 31, 1833, and ordained an apostle on April 26, 1839. In his early years he worked as a miller and attended school. He served two missions to England and was the Church historian for 23 years. Throughout his life he kept a detailed, multivolumed diary. In 1895 President Woodruff recorded that he had traveled 172,369 miles, attended 7,655 meetings, given 3,526 talks, confirmed 8,952 people, received 18,977 letters, and written 11,519 letters. Fishing and farming were two passions of his life.

WILFORD WOODRUFF ABOUT 1860

Following President Taylor's death, Elder Woodruff presided over the Church as president of the Twelve until he was made president of the Church in April 1889. He pushed the completion of the Salt Lake Temple and presided at its April 1893 dedication. President Woodruff died at the home of Isaac Trumbo in San Francisco on September 2, 1898.

RECONCILIATION

THE MANIFESTO AND AMNESTY

President Wilford Woodruff, fearing for the temporal salvation of the Church, "wrestled mightily with the Lord." On September 24, 1890, he issued the Manifesto, announcing the official end to polygamy. The Manifesto brought the Church cooperation and reconciliation. It also marked the end of Church isolation and the beginning of increased integration into American society.

On January 4, 1893, President Benjamin Harrison issued an amnesty to Saints who had entered polygamy before November 1, 1890. The amnesty was made more general in 1894. President Grover Cleveland signed a resolution to return confiscated property to the Church; the real estate was not returned for three years.

LORENZO SNOW (1814–1901)

Lorenzo Snow was a student at Oberlin College when he decided to join the Church. Baptized in June 1836, he served missions in England, Italy, and Switzerland. He was ordained an apostle in February 1849, and in 1853 he organized the Brigham City Mercantile and Manufacturing Association. From March 1886 to February 1887 he was imprisoned for polygamy.

LORENZO SNOW ABOUT 1860

When Lorenzo Snow became president on September 13, 1898, the Church was close to financial ruin. It owed more than $1.25 million. This terrible situation was caused by the federal government's confiscation of Church property, a drop in tithing receipts, and borrowing money.

To end the debt, the First Presidency cut expenditures, consolidated debts, offered two $500,000 bonds, sold nonessential property, quit borrowing money for investments, and urged the Saints to increase contributions. In May 1899 President Snow, at the St. George Tabernacle, said, "This is the answer to our financial problems. . . . If this people will pay a full and honest tithing, the shackles of indebtedness will be removed from us."

President Snow died of pneumonia on October 10, 1901. His financial undertakings allowed the Church to be debt-free by 1907. During his presidency the Church grew by 10 stakes and 25,680 members.

STATEHOOD

The U.S. Congress denied Utah's first six applications for statehood over the issues of polygamy and LDS church control of local politics. It took 49 years and the abandonment of polygamy in 1890 to pave the way for statehood 6 years later.

But events in the previous decades ensured the end of Mormon isolationism in their mountain stronghold: U.S. soldiers stationed in Utah, the influx of non-Mormon prospectors and merchants, and the completion of the Transcontinental Railroad in 1869 tied Utah to America's social and political life. The Church continued to influence the state, but Utahns also began to view themselves as Americans with loyalties to its institutions and traditions. President Grover Cleveland finally signed the law making Utah a state on January 4, 1896.

ENDOWMENT HOUSE

The Endowment House stood on the northwest corner of the Salt Lake Temple block from 1855 until 1889. As its name implies, sacred temple ordinances were performed there while the Saints built the temple.

Before the Nauvoo Temple was completed, Joseph Smith used the upper room of his red-brick store to confer the first temple ordinances (endowments). After arriving in the Salt Lake Valley, Brigham Young used Ensign Peak as a "natural temple." Between 1851 and 1855, 2,200 ordinances took place in the upper chambers of the Salt Lake Council House.

The Endowment House, dedicated May 5, 1855, measured 34 feet by 44 feet. It was a two-story structure with one-story extensions on each end. More than 54,000 endowments were performed there before the building was torn down in November 1889.

ST. GEORGE TEMPLE

Brigham Young chose the site for the St. George Temple in 1871. It was the first temple completed in Utah and also the first one built free of harassment from enemies. Built with local materials and crafted by pioneer artisans, it was an example of the self-sufficiency that President Young wanted for the Saints. Brigham Young presided over its April 6–8, 1877, dedication. Shortly after the dedication, the original spire was destroyed by fire and replaced by a taller one.

Temple endowments for the dead were first introduced at this temple, and baptism for the dead was reintroduced for the first time since Nauvoo.

A beautiful white "Castellated Gothic" structure made of native sandstone, its dimensions are 142 feet long, 96 feet wide, 80 feet high, and 175 feet to the top of vane. Truman O. Angell was the architect. The cost was approximately $800,000. The original building was 56,062 square feet; it was increased to 110,000 square feet after remodeling in 1975.

LOGAN TEMPLE

The Logan Temple was the second temple completed in Utah. Brigham Young chose its site, and ground was broken on May 18, 1877. The Saints experienced a great outpouring of the Spirit at the May 17, 1884, dedicatory services conducted by John Taylor. Much of the temple was built during the beginnings of the heavy anti-polygamy persecution. Craftsmen wrote pro-Mormon and pro-polygamy statements on the plaster in the ceiling.

Built with dark-colored limestone, its dimensions are 171 feet long, 95 feet wide, and 86 feet high; the west tower is 165 feet high. Truman O. Angell was the architect. It cost $750,000 to build. Originally 59,130 square feet, it was 115,507 square feet after remodeling in 1979.

MANTI TEMPLE

The site for the Manti Temple was chosen by Brigham Young on June 25, 1875, but construction did not begin until 1877. In hiding from federal prosecutors, President Wilford Woodruff conducted private dedicatory ceremonies on May 17, 1888. Three public dedications were held May 21–23 with Elder Lorenzo Snow reading the prayer.

Built with cream-colored limestone, the temple's dimensions are 171 feet long, 95 feet wide, and 86 feet high; the tower is 179 feet high. William F. Folsom was the architect. It cost $993,000 to build. It totals 86,809 square feet.

THE SITE

On July 28, 1847, four days after arriving in the Salt Lake Valley, Brigham Young walked with the Twelve to a spot between two creeks, waved his hand, tapped his walking stick on the ground, and said, "Here we will build the temple of our God."

In the early stages of designing the temple, several building materials were considered, including adobe, which Brigham Young thought might harden with time. By the time temple construction began on February 14, 1853, architects Truman Angell and William Weeks had decided to use sandstone for the footings and foundation. The foundation was completed in 1855. In 1858, with the threat of advancing U.S. troops, the Saints evacuated Salt Lake City and buried the temple foundation, disguising it as a plowed field. When construction resumed, workers discovered flaws in the foundation. On January 1, 1862, Brigham Young announced that the entire temple would be built with granite. Masons and stonecutters reset the foundation, supplementing the sandstone with granite from Little Cottonwood Creek.

TRUMAN O. ANGELL (1810–1887)

A builder from Rhode Island, Truman Angell was a construction supervisor on the Kirtland Temple. He came to Utah in 1847. In 1853 Brigham Young, his brother-in-law, chose him to be the Church architect. He was sent on a mission to England to study architecture. Under his guidance the Salt Lake Temple, St. George Temple, Salt Lake Tabernacle, and Logan Temple were built.

ART MISSIONARIES

In 1890 four "art missionaries" arrived in Paris, France, to study art at the Julian Academy. The Church paid for their travel and study in exchange for artistic services when they returned to Utah. The beautiful Salt Lake Temple murals are a result of this inspired arrangement. Paris provided an artistic atmosphere that was experimental and exciting. The city was still the hotbed of Impressionism. The four missionaries were John B. Fairbanks (1855–1940), Lorus Pratt (1855–1923), John Hafen (1857–1910), and Edwin Evans (1860–1946). Herman Haag (1871–1895) joined them in 1891. The lessons these artists learned in Paris influenced the Utah art scene for years.

COMPLETION

By 1867 the Saints saw the Salt Lake Temple's granite walls emerging above ground level. The construction was progressing steadily if not quickly. The heavy granite was hard to transport. Each trip to the quarry took four days out and back. The pioneers tried using a canal, a wooden railway, and a specially designed heavy-load wagon. The problem was solved with the laying of a railroad spur to the canyon for mining.

The temple took 40 years to complete. For the Saints it was an effort filled with sacrifice, commitment, and perseverance. Many carpenters, masons, stonecutters, and artisans participated in the venture. At any given time, 150 men worked on the temple.

On April 6, 1892, 50,000 people witnessed the laying of the capstone ceremony. Later that day a 12-foot, gold-leafed statue of Angel Moroni was anchored onto the capstone on the central eastern tower.

One year later, on April 6, 1893, the temple was dedicated—46 years after Brigham Young chose the site. With 2,250 people gathered in the fourth-floor assembly room, President Wilford Woodruff gave the dedicatory prayer. In all there were 31 dedicatory sessions from April 6 to April 24.

The temples dimensions are: 181 feet long, 118 feet wide, 107 feet high; the east center tower is 210 feet high; the west center tower is 204 feet high. The exterior walls are 8 feet thick at the base and 6 feet thick at the top. The cost was approximately $4 million.

CHURCH HISTORY TIME LINE
(1820–1900)

The Church history time line begins with Joseph Smith and the First Vision (1820). It covers the Restoration, Kirtland and Missouri (1831–1839), Nauvoo (1839–1846), pioneers (1846–1869), and the struggles over polygamy and its resolution. The time line ends with the dedication of the Salt Lake Temple and the Church entering a new century.

LEGEND

Joseph Smith —————— • **June** Joseph moves to
Fayette, New York

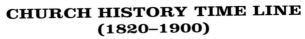

Major Events —————— **Spring, 1820** The First Vision (p. 2)
from Joseph's life

Persecution —————— ✹ **September** Saints forced out of
of the Saints Clay County, Missouri; they settle
in Caldwell County, Missouri

Events in Iowa —————— • **April 24** Camp at
and Nebraska Garden Grove, Iowa

Dedication —————— • **March 27** Kirtland
of Temples Temple dedicated
(p. 11)

Birth of —————— • **November 13**
Prophets Joseph F. Smith born,
son of Hyrum Smith

CHURCH PRESIDENTS
TIME LINE (1820–PRESENT)

The biographical boxes and the time line are color-coded to match each president with the years and events of his administration. Major milestones in the growth of the Church, such as Church membership, missionary numbers, and temples, are highlighted.

LEGEND

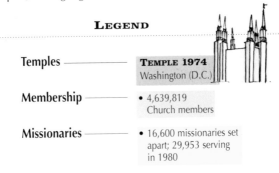

Temples —————— **TEMPLE 1974** Washington (D.C.)

Membership —————— • 4,639,819
Church members

Missionaries —————— • 16,600 missionaries set
apart; 29,953 serving
in 1980

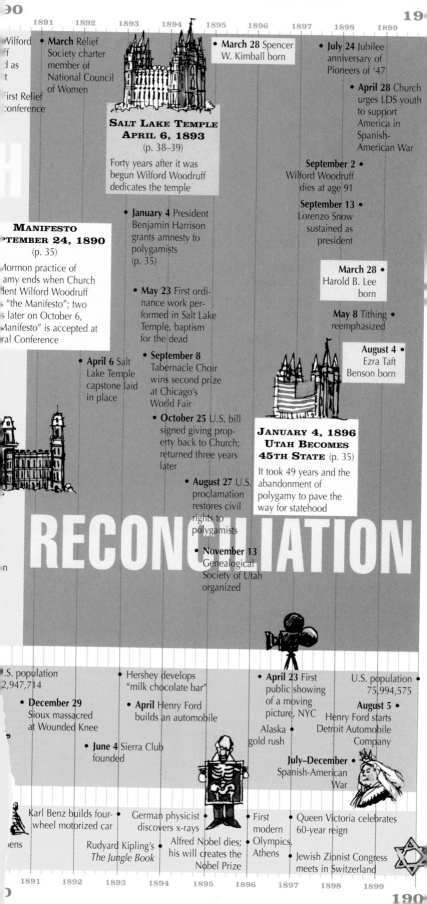

Wilford
ff
d as
t

First Relief
conference

• **March** Relief Society charter member of National Council of Women

March 28 Spencer W. Kimball born

• **July 24** Jubilee anniversary of Pioneers of '47

• **April 28** Church urges LDS youth to support America in Spanish-American War

SALT LAKE TEMPLE APRIL 6, 1893
(p. 38–39)

Forty years after it was begun Wilford Woodruff dedicates the temple

September 2 •
Wilford Woodruff dies at age 91

September 13 •
Lorenzo Snow sustained as president

• **January 4** President Benjamin Harrison grants amnesty to polygamists (p. 35)

MANIFESTO
PTEMBER 24, 1890
(p. 35)

Mormon practice of
amy ends when Church
lent Wilford Woodruff
"the Manifesto"; two
s later on October 6,
Manifesto" is accepted at
ral Conference

• **May 23** First ordinance work performed in Salt Lake Temple, baptism for the dead

March 28 •
Harold B. Lee born

May 8 Tithing •
reemphasized

August 4 •
Ezra Taft Benson born

• **April 6** Salt Lake Temple capstone laid in place

• **September 8** Tabernacle Choir wins second prize at Chicago's World Fair

• **October 25** U.S. bill signed giving property back to Church; returned three years later

JANUARY 4, 1896 UTAH BECOMES 45TH STATE (p. 35)

It took 49 years and the abandonment of polygamy to pave the way for statehood

• **August 27** U.S. proclamation restores civil rights to polygamists

• **November 13** Genealogical Society of Utah organized

RECONCILIATION

.S. population
2,947,714

• **December 29** Sioux massacred at Wounded Knee

• **June 4** Sierra Club founded

• Hershey develops "milk chocolate bar"

• **April** Henry Ford builds an automobile

• **April 23** First public showing of a moving picture, NYC

Alaska gold rush

July–December •
Spanish-American War

U.S. population •
75,994,575

August 5 •
Henry Ford starts Detroit Automobile Company

Karl Benz builds four-wheel motorized car

German physicist discovers x-rays

Rudyard Kipling's *The Jungle Book*

Alfred Nobel dies; his will creates the Nobel Prize

First modern Olympics, Athens

• Queen Victoria celebrates 60-year reign

• Jewish Zionist Congress meets in Switzerland

| 1881 | 1882 | 1883 | 1884 | 1885 | 1886 | 1887 | 1888 | 1889 |

- **October 10** John Taylor sustained president of the Church; Pearl of Great Price accepted as scripture

- **January 8** Assembly Hall on Temple Square dedicated

- **March 22** Edmunds anti-polygamy bill signed into law (p. 32)

POLYGAMY
(p. 32–33)

From 1882 until the 1890 "Manifesto," federal officials wage an all-out campaign to prosecute and jail Mormon polygamists

- **July 17** Deseret Hospital opened by Relief Society

- **August 18** Utah Commission arrives in Utah to enforce disenfranchisement of polygamists (p. 33)

- **May 17** Logan Temple dedicated (p. 37)

- **August 10** Mob murders Elders Berry and Gibbs in Tennessee

- **September 1** Callous judge Charles Zane assigned to Utah's 3rd District Court; convicts hundreds of polygamists

- **November 3** In a polygamy test case Rudger Clawson receives a four-year prison sentence; 1,035 Utahns will be imprisoned for polygamy

- **February 1** John Taylor delivers his last speech in the Tabernacle; he and other leaders go into hiding

- **February 3** Idaho law prohibits all Mormons from voting

- **May 13** Utah delegation meets with Pres. Cleveland, presents "Statement of Grievances and Protest" concerning anti-polygamy injustices

- **December 26** Thomas L. Kane, the Mormons' friend, dies

- **January 31** First LDS meetinghouse in Mexico at Colonia Juarez

- **March 6** 2,000 LDS women meet to protest federal abuse

- **February 17–18** Edmunds-Tucker Act becomes law (p. 32)

- **June 3** Alberta, Canada settled

- **July 25** John Taylor dies at age 78; Twelve assumes leadership

- **July 30** U.S. files suit against Church; property confiscated

- **November** U.S. government rents back to the Church some of its own property, including the temple block

- **January 25** David Whitmer dies (p. 5)

- **May 17-21** Manti Temple dedicated (p. 37)

- **June 8** Stakes instructed to establish academies; 32 established by 1910

- **September 17** George Q. Cannon enters prison for polygamy

- **April 7** Woodruff sustained president

- **April 6** Society held

SE

The poly... Presi... issue... week... "the Gene...

population 5,783

- **July 14** Billy the Kid killed

- **October 26** Gunfight at the O.K. Corral

ski

- **December 25** First electrically lit Christmas tree

- **March 24** Telephone service between New York and Chicago established

World's first "skyscraper" in Chicago

First Sherlock Holmes story, A Study in Scarlet

Belgium hosts first beauty contest

- **October 28** Statue of Liberty dedicated

- First simple, inexpensive camera introduced

- First U.S. golf club, St. Andrews, Yonkers, New York

Jack the Ripper terrorizes London

Eiffel To... in Paris

| 1881 | 1882 | 1883 | 1884 | 1885 | 1886 | 1887 | 1888 | 1889 |

JOSEPH SMITH

BORN	December 23, 1805, at Sharon, Vermont
MARRIED	January 18, 1827, to Emma Hale
RECEIVED	May/June 1829, Aaronic and Melchizedek Priesthood (ordained an apostle), age 23
SUSTAINED	April 6, 1830, First Elder of the Church, age 24
ORDAINED	June 3, 1831, high priest, age 25
SUSTAINED	January 25, 1832, President of the High Priesthood, age 26
MARTYRED	June 27, 1844, at Carthage, Illinois, age 38

"The Spirit of Revelation is . . . pure intelligence flowing."

BRIGHAM YOU

BORN	June 1, 1801, at Whitingham, Ve
MARRIED	October 5, 1824, Miriam Works (die September 1832) February 18, 1834 Ann Angell
APOSTLE	February 14, 1835
PRESIDENT	December 27, 18 age 46
DIED	August 29, 1877, Lake City, age 76

"Mormonism embraces all tr

- **Spring** The First Vision (p. 2)

- **September 21-22** Angel Moroni visits Joseph (p. 4)

- **April 6** Church organized (p. 7)

- **September 22** Joseph receives gold plates of Book of Mormon

- **May 15** Aaronic Priesthood restored (p. 6)

- **May or June** Melchizedek Priesthood restored (p. 6)

- **March** First edition of Book of Mormon published

- **June** Samuel Smith, first missionary

- **December 31** 280 Church members

- 16 missionaries set apart in 1830

- **September–October** Missionaries called to Lamanites (p. 16)

- **June 3-6** First high priest ordained

- **January 25** Joseph sustained president of high priests

- **February 4** Edward Partridge, first bishop (p. 10)

- **August 3** Missouri temple site dedicated (p. 10)

- **June** Elders sent to Canada—first missionaries outside US

- First issue of *The Evening and the Morning Star*, Independence, then Kirtland (until 1834)

- **March 18** First Presidency organized

- **December 18** Joseph Smith, Sr, first Church Patriarch (p. 3)

- **February 17** First high council organized (D&C 102)

- **October** *Messenger and Advocate* begins publication, Kirtland (until 1837)

- **February 14** Twelve apostles chosen (p. 11)

- **February 28** First Quorum of Seventy organized

- **August 17** Doctrine and Covenants accepted as one of Standard Works (p. 9)

TEMPLE 1836 Kirtland (p. 11)

- **July** First missio in Great Britain

- **October** *Elder's Journal* begins p cation, Kirtland 1838)

- **May** Missi

- **Nove** *Seaso* catio 1846)

| 1820 | 1822 | 1824 | 1826 | 1828 | 1830 | 1832 | 1834 | 1836 | 1838 | 184 |

JOHN TAYLOR

BORN	November 1, 1808, at Milnthorp, England
MARRIED	January 28, 1833, to Leonora Cannon
APOSTLE	December 19, 1838, age 30
PRESIDENT	October 10, 1880, age 71
DIED	July 25, 1887, at Kaysville, Utah, age 78

"The Kingdom of God or nothing."

WILFORD WOODRUFF

BORN	March 1, 1807, a[t] Farmington, Conn[.]
MARRIED	April 13, 1837, to Whitmore Carter
APOSTLE	April 26, 1839, ag[e]
PRESIDENT	April 7, 1889, age
DIED	September 2, 189[ ] Francisco, age 91

"The Lord is with us and gives us re[ ]

- **May 11** Scandinavian Mission organized

- 50 missionaries set apart in 1850

- 51,839 Church members

- **August 29** Doctrine of polygamy publicly announced (p. 32)

- 96 missionaries set apart in 1860

- 61,082 Church members

- **July 8** US declares p[ ] a crime

  Nover[ ] Retr[ ] formed W[ ]

---

sue of
[s]*tar*,
England

ries
1840
rch

- **May 3** *Nauvoo Neighbor* begins publication, Kirtland (for 2 ½ years)

[M]ay 4 Temple endow[m]ent first given

- **April 30** Society Islands Mission organized

- **December 15** Welsh Mission organized

TEMPLE 1846 Nauvoo (p. 19)

- **July 24** First pioneers enter Salt Lake Valley (p. 22)

ates
[ ]d

[ ] and
[ ]ubli-
[ ]ntil

MORMON TRA[IL]

MAP LEGEND
- EARLY CHURCH MOVEMENT AND GATHERING (1805–1846)
- THE MORMON PIONEER TRAIL (1846–1869)
- MORMON BATTALION (1846–1847)
- POINTS OF INTEREST

INDEPENDENCE ROCK · DEVIL'S GATE · FT. LARAMIE · FT. BRIDGER · CHIMNEY ROCK · NORTH PLATTE · WINTER QUARTERS · CO[ ] BL[ ] · FT. KEARNEY · SACRAMENTO · ★ SALT LAKE CITY · SAN FRANCISCO · FT. LEAVENWORTH · SANTA FE · LOS ANGELES · SAN DIEGO · YUMA · TUCSON

January 1 First issue of *Mormon Tribune* (*Salt Lake Tribune*)

February 12 Utah Territorial legislature gives women the vote

April 4 George Albert Smith born

March 2 Apostle George A. Smith prays at Mount of Olives

September 8 David O. McKay born

June 2 100 Gosiute Indians baptized

October 26 • George Reynolds indicted and becomes test case for polygamy laws (p. 32)

Winter • United Orders begin (p. 29)

February Ann Eliza Webb sues Brigham Young for divorce

March 20 Approximately 200 Shivwits Indians baptized

May 14 First "Old Folks' Day" held at Lake Point, Great Salt Lake

June 10 Young Men's Mutual Improvement Association organized

July 10 Martin Harris dies (p. 5)

October 9 Salt Lake Tabernacle dedicated (p. 27)

October 16 Brigham Young Academy founded (later BYU) (p. 30)

March 23 LDS colonization of Arizona begins

July 14 Sidney Rigdon dies (p. 19)

March 23 John D. Lee executed for part in Mountain Meadows Massacre

April 6 St. George Temple dedicated (p. 36)

April 6 Massive organizing of stakes in Utah

May 19 First L settlement in Colorado

August 25 founded by Rogers (p.

Janua Supre upho Anti-(p. 32

Ap Ha Bi age

June 11 Methodists hold Utah's first "camp meeting"

October 2 Brigham Young arrested for bigamy; confined to home

January 2 Brigham Young appears in court; remains in home custody

April 25 Brigham Young released from custody

DEATH OF BRIGHAM YOUNG AUGUST 29, 1877 (p. 31)
Utah goes into mourning; 25,000 attend viewing

ovember 28 ung Ladies' trenchment sociation med (p. 29)

ecember Ex-ormon Godbeite ovement begins

CMI usiness

July 19 Joseph Fielding Smith born

September 4 Quorum of Twelve assume leadership

October 8 Great Chicago Fire

ovember 6 First inter-llegiate football game

March 1 Yellowstone National Park created

U.S. population 39,818,449

Mark Twain's *The Adventures of Tom Sawyer*

• U.S. centennial

March 7 Alexander Graham Bell patents the telephone

June 25 Custer's forces annihilated at "Little Big Horn"

Octo Thom inver

December Thomas patents the phonogr

opens
1870–1871 Franco-Prussian War

• Jules Verne's *Around the World in 80 Days*

• First roller-skating rink, London

• "Impressionist" art exhibition, in Paris

• German Karl Ber builds motorized tricycle

• First race,

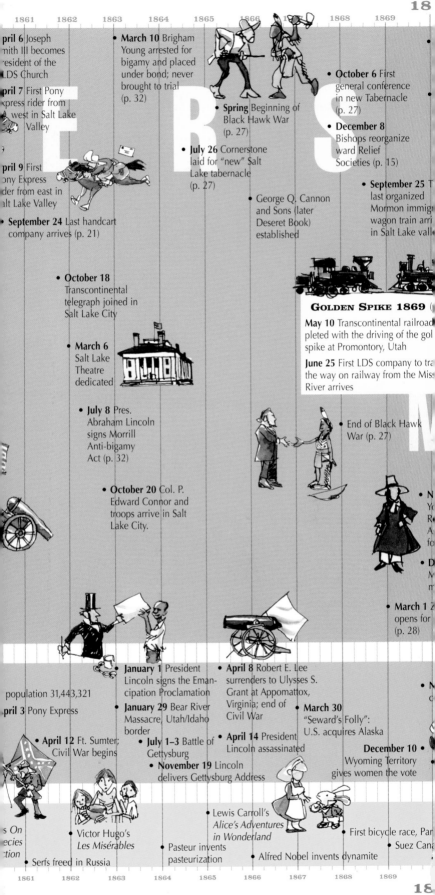

1861 1862 1863 1864 1865 1866 1867 1868 1869

pril 6 Joseph mith III becomes resident of the LDS Church

pril 7 First Pony xpress rider from west in Salt Lake Valley

pril 9 First ony Express der from east in alt Lake Valley

• **September 24** Last handcart company arrives (p. 21)

• **March 10** Brigham Young arrested for bigamy and placed under bond; never brought to trial (p. 32)

• **Spring** Beginning of Black Hawk War (p. 27)

• **July 26** Cornerstone laid for "new" Salt Lake tabernacle (p. 27)

• George Q. Cannon and Sons (later Deseret Book) established

• **October 6** First general conference in new Tabernacle (p. 27)

• **December 8** Bishops reorganize ward Relief Societies (p. 15)

• **September 25** T last organized Mormon immigr wagon train arri in Salt Lake vall

GOLDEN SPIKE 1869 (

May 10 Transcontinental railroad pleted with the driving of the gol spike at Promontory, Utah

June 25 First LDS company to tra the way on railway from the Miss River arrives

• **October 18** Transcontinental telegraph joined in Salt Lake City

• **March 6** Salt Lake Theatre dedicated

• **July 8** Pres. Abraham Lincoln signs Morrill Anti-bigamy Act (p. 32)

• **October 20** Col. P. Edward Connor and troops arrive in Salt Lake City.

• End of Black Hawk War (p. 27)

• N Y R A fo

• D M m

• **March 1** Z opens for (p. 28)

population 31,443,321

pril 3 Pony Express

• **April 12** Ft. Sumter; Civil War begins

• **January 1** President Lincoln signs the Emancipation Proclamation

• **January 29** Bear River Massacre, Utah/Idaho border

• **July 1–3** Battle of Gettysburg

• **November 19** Lincoln delivers Gettysburg Address

• **April 8** Robert E. Lee surrenders to Ulysses S. Grant at Appomattox, Virginia; end of Civil War

• **April 14** President Lincoln assassinated

• **March 30** "Seward's Folly": U.S. acquires Alaska

• N d

• **December 10** • Wyoming Territory gives women the vote

s On ecies tion

• Serfs freed in Russia

• Victor Hugo's Les Misérables

• Pasteur invents pasteurization

• Lewis Carroll's Alice's Adventures in Wonderland

• Alfred Nobel invents dynamite

• First bicycle race, Par

• Suez Cana

1861 1862 1863 1864 1865 1866 1867 1868 1869

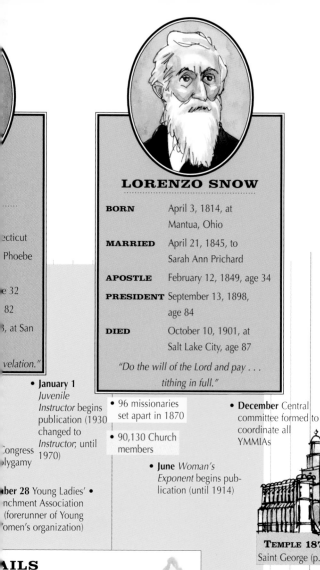

LORENZO SNOW

BORN	April 3, 1814, at Mantua, Ohio
MARRIED	April 21, 1845, to Sarah Ann Prichard
APOSTLE	February 12, 1849, age 34
PRESIDENT	September 13, 1898, age 84
DIED	October 10, 1901, at Salt Lake City, age 87

"Do the will of the Lord and pay . . . tithing in full."

JOSEPH F

BORN	Novem at Far V
MARRIED	May 5, Lambsc
APOSTLE	July 1,
PRESIDENT	Octobe
DIED	Novem Salt Lak

"There is no salvatic of Go

ecticut

Phoebe

e 32

82

3, at San

velation."

- **January 1** *Juvenile Instructor* begins publication (1930 changed to *Instructor*, until 1970)

Congress
lygamy

ber 28 Young Ladies' •
nchment Association
(forerunner of Young
omen's organization)

- 96 missionaries set apart in 1870
- 90,130 Church members

- **June** *Woman's Exponent* begins publication (until 1914)

- **December** Central committee formed to coordinate all YMMIAs

February 17–
Edmunds-Tucker A
becomes law (p. 3

TEMPLE 1877
Saint George (p. 36)

- **August 25** Primary founded (p. 30)

- **June 10** Young Men's Mutual Improvement Association organized

- **October 4** *Contributor* begins publication (until 1896)

- 219 missionaries set apart in 1880
- 133,628 Church members

- **March 22** Edmunds Antipolygamy bill signed into law (p. 32)

TEMPLE 1
Logan (p.

- Presi
  and •
  leade
  (p. 3

AILS

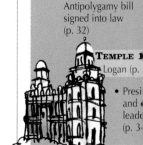

SHARON

PALMYRA

KIRTLAND

JNCIL
FFS

NAUVOO

INDEPENDENCE

1866   1868   **1870**   1872   1874   1876   1878   **1880**   1882   1884   188

SMITH

BORN	April 1738, ouri
	ulina
	27
	, age 62
	18, at
	e 80

e way

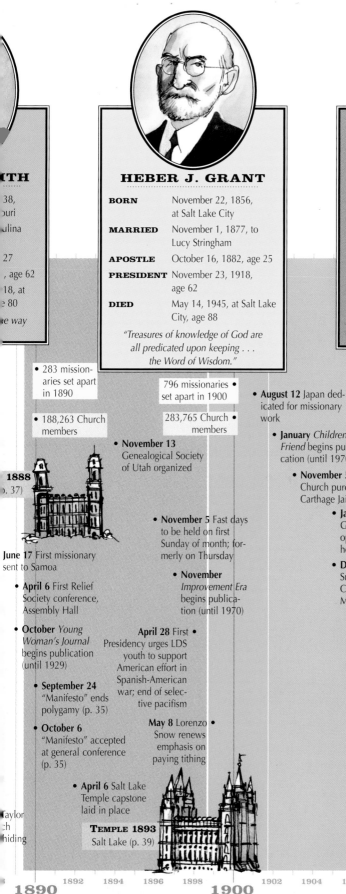

HEBER J. GRANT

BORN	November 22, 1856, at Salt Lake City
MARRIED	November 1, 1877, to Lucy Stringham
APOSTLE	October 16, 1882, age 25
PRESIDENT	November 23, 1918, age 62
DIED	May 14, 1945, at Salt Lake City, age 88

"Treasures of knowledge of God are
all predicated upon keeping . . .
the Word of Wisdom."

GEORGE
SMI

BORN	April at Salt
MARRIED	May 2 Emily
APOSTLE	Octob
PRESIDENT	May 2
DIED	April City, a

"I would be a frienc

• 933 missionaries
set apart in 1910

398,478 Church
members

Church ado
Boy Scout progr

• 283 mission-
aries set apart
in 1890

796 missionaries •
set apart in 1900

• **August 12** Japan dedicated for missionary
work

• 188,263 Church
members

283,765 Church •
members

• **January** *Children's*
Friend begins publi-
cation (until 1970)

• **November 13**
Genealogical Society
of Utah organized

• **November 5** The
Church purchases
Carthage Jail

1888
). 37)

• **January 1** Dr. William
Groves LDS hospital
opens, first in Church
hospital system

• **November 5** Fast days
to be held on first
Sunday of month; for-
merly on Thursday

June 17 First missionary
sent to Samoa

• **December 23** Joseph
Smith Memorial
Cottage and
Monument dedicated

• **November**
Improvement Era
begins publica-
tion (until 1970)

• **April 6** First Relief
Society conference,
Assembly Hall

• **Summer** President
Joseph F. Smith vis
Europe—first presi-
dent to do so

• **October** *Young*
Woman's Journal
begins publication
(until 1929)

April 28 First •
Presidency urges LDS
youth to support
American effort in
Spanish-American
war; end of selec-
tive pacifism

• **February** U.S.
Senate agrees
seat Utah sena
(and apostle) F
Smoot

• **September 24**
"Manifesto" ends
polygamy (p. 35)

May 8 Lorenzo •
Snow renews
emphasis on
paying tithing

• **April 8** C
Priesthoc
Committe
created (

• **October 6**
"Manifesto" accepted
at general conference
(p. 35)

• **April 6** Salt Lake
Temple capstone
laid in place

aylor
:h
hiding

TEMPLE 1893
Salt Lake (p. 39)

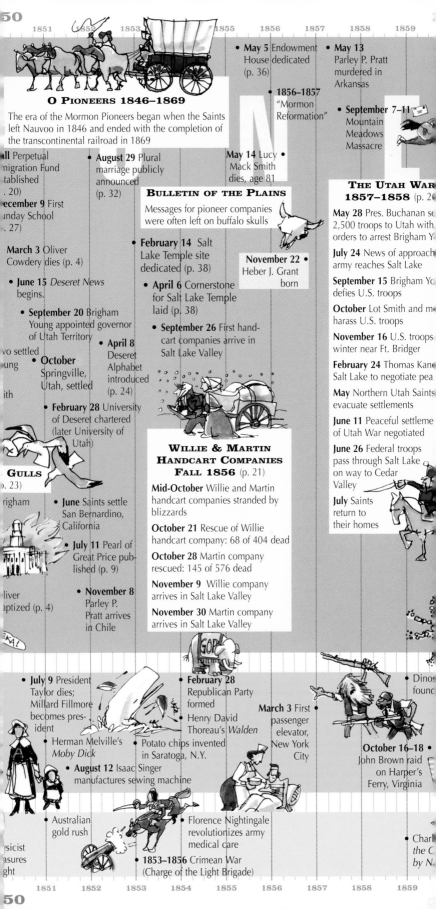

1851   1852   1853   1854   1855   1856   1857   1858   1859

O PIONEERS 1846–1869

The era of the Mormon Pioneers began when the Saints left Nauvoo in 1846 and ended with the completion of the transcontinental railroad in 1869

- **May 5** Endowment House dedicated (p. 36)

- **1856–1857** "Mormon Reformation"

- **May 13** Parley P. Pratt murdered in Arkansas

- **September 7–11** Mountain Meadows Massacre

...ll Perpetual ...migration Fund ...tablished (. 20)

- **August 29** Plural marriage publicly announced (p. 32)

...ecember 9 First ...unday School (. 27)

May 14 Lucy • Mack Smith dies, age 81

BULLETIN OF THE PLAINS

Messages for pioneer companies were often left on buffalo skulls

THE UTAH WAR 1857–1858 (p. 2...

May 28 Pres. Buchanan se... 2,500 troops to Utah with orders to arrest Brigham Y...

March 3 Oliver Cowdery dies (p. 4)

- **June 15** *Deseret News* begins.

- **September 20** Brigham Young appointed governor of Utah Territory

- **February 14** Salt Lake Temple site dedicated (p. 38)

- **April 6** Cornerstone for Salt Lake Temple laid (p. 38)

- **September 26** First handcart companies arrive in Salt Lake Valley

November 22 • Heber J. Grant born

July 24 News of approach... army reaches Salt Lake

September 15 Brigham Yo... defies U.S. troops

October Lot Smith and m... harass U.S. troops

November 16 U.S. troops ... winter near Ft. Bridger

...vo settled ...ung

- **October** Springville, Utah, settled

- **April 8** Deseret Alphabet introduced (p. 24)

...ith

- **February 28** University of Deseret chartered (later University of Utah)

February 24 Thomas Kane ... Salt Lake to negotiate pea...

May Northern Utah Saints ... evacuate settlements

June 11 Peaceful settleme... of Utah War negotiated

WILLIE & MARTIN HANDCART COMPANIES FALL 1856 (p. 21)

Mid-October Willie and Martin handcart companies stranded by blizzards

October 21 Rescue of Willie handcart company: 68 of 404 dead

October 28 Martin company rescued: 145 of 576 dead

November 9 Willie company arrives in Salt Lake Valley

November 30 Martin company arrives in Salt Lake Valley

June 26 Federal troops pass through Salt Lake on way to Cedar Valley

July Saints return to their homes

GULLS
(. 23)

...righam

- **June** Saints settle San Bernardino, California

- **July 11** Pearl of Great Price published (p. 9)

...liver ...aptized (p. 4)

- **November 8** Parley P. Pratt arrives in Chile

- **July 9** President Taylor dies; Millard Fillmore becomes president

- Herman Melville's *Moby Dick*

- **August 12** Isaac Singer manufactures sewing machine

- **February 28** Republican Party formed

- Henry David Thoreau's *Walden*

- Potato chips invented in Saratoga, N.Y.

March 3 First • passenger elevator, New York City

- Dino... found...

October 16–18 • John Brown raid on Harper's Ferry, Virginia

- Australian gold rush

- Florence Nightingale revolutionizes army medical care

- **1853–1856** Crimean War (Charge of the Light Brigade)

...ysicist ...asures ...ght

- Charl... the C... by N...

1841 • 1842 • 1843 • 1844 • 1845 • 1846 • 1847 • 1848 • 1849

leave
)

• **January 19** Command to build Nauvoo Temple (D&C 124) (p. 19)

• **August 7** Joseph Smith's brother Don Carlos dies

oseph moves p. 14)

er 29
leaves for ngton, D.C.

rch 4 Joseph k in Nauvoo

• **October 24** Orson Hyde dedicates Palestine (p. 16)

• **March 1** Articles of Faith and Joseph Smith's history published

• **March 17** Relief Society organized (p. 15)

• **August 15** "Baptism for the Dead" revealed

• **September 14** Joseph Smith Sr. dies, age 69

• **December 16** Gov. Thomas Carlin signs "Nauvoo Charter" (p. 14)

• **July 12** Revelation on eternal marriage (D&C 132)

• **January 29** Joseph Smith candidate for U.S. president

• **April 7** Joseph Smith gives King Follett discourse

• **June 7** *Nauvoo Expositor* published (p. 18)

• **June 10** *Nauvoo Expositor* destroyed (p. 18)

• **May 4** First temple endowment

• **May 4** Attempted murder of Gov. Boggs, Mormons accused

• **August 6** Joseph prophesies the Saints will settle in the Rocky Mountains

CARTHAGE JAIL 1844 (p. 18)

June 25 Joseph and Hyrum Smith surrender themselves; imprisoned in Carthage jail

June 27 Mob forces way inside and murders Joseph and Hyrum

July 30 Joseph's brother Samuel dies

August 6 Brigham Young arrives in Nauvoo from Boston

August 8 Mantle of prophet upon Brigham Young (p. 19)

November 17 Widow Emma Smith gives birth to David Hyrum Smith

laid

• **January** Nauvoo charter repealed by Illinois legislature

• **May 30** Assassins of Joseph and Hyrum Smith acquitted

• **February 4** Saints begin crossing the Mississippi (p. 20)

• **February 4** Ship *Brooklyn* leaves New York (p. 22)

• **April 24** Camp at Garden Grove, Iowa

• **May 1** Nauvoo Temple dedicated (p. 19)

• **May 18** Encampment at Mt. Pisgah, Iowa

June Thomas Kane visits Saints (p. 26)

June 30 U.S. army asks 500 enlistees (p. 21)

June 14 Encampment at Council Bluffs

July 16 Mormon Battalion begins 2,000-mile march (p. 21)

July 29 Ship *Brooklyn* arrives in San Francisco (p. 22)

• **September 23** Saints at Winter Quarters

September 12 Battle of Nauvoo; remaining Saints driven out

• **January 14** Saints organize trek west (D&C 136)

• **April 5** First companies leave Winter Quarters

• **July 16** Mormon Battalion discharged at Los Angeles

• **July 21** Orson Pratt and Erastus Snow enter Great Salt Lake Valley (p. 22)

THIS IS THE PLACE JULY 24, 1847 (p. 22)

Brigham Young enters valley with first wagon companies

• **July 28** Site for Temple selected (p. 38)

• **August** Brigham Young leaves for Winter Quarters

• **March** Pr

• **December 5** Brigham Y sustained as president

• **December 23** Emma Sm marries Lewis Bidamon

• **January 24** Mormon battalion members at Sutter's Mill

MIRACLE OF TH JUNE 1848

• **September 20** Young in Salt Lake Valley

• **October 9** Nauvoo Temple burns to ground

• **November** Cowdery re

• **F** E

• **D** S (

S. population ,069,453

• First large group (48 wagons) migrates over Oregon Trail to California

NEVERMORE!

day or

Edgar Allen Poe's *The Raven and Other Poems*

uis Daguerre introduces t usable photographic process

• **May 24** Samuel F. B. Morse sends first telegraph message

3,000 immigrants follow the Oregon Trail to Oregon

Charles Dickens' *A Christmas Carol*

Potato famine in Ireland

• **1846-1848** Mexican War

• **January 24** Gold discovered near Sutter's Mill, California

U.S. population 23,191,876

Nathaniel Hawthorne's *The Scarlet Letter*

Charlotte Bronte's *Jane Eyre*

Emily Bronte's *Wuthering Heights*

Marx and Engels' *The Communist Manifesto*

• French p Fizeau m speed of

ALBERT
[SMI]TH

, 1870,
[Salt] Lake City

, 1892, to Lucy
[Woo]druff

[Octobe]r 8, 1903, age 33

, 1945, age 75

, 1951, at Salt Lake
[a]ge 81

to the friendless."

DAVID O. McKAY

BORN	September 8, 1873, at Huntsville, Utah
MARRIED	January 2, 1901, to Emma Ray Riggs
APOSTLE	April 9, 1906, age 32
PRESIDENT	April 9, 1951, age 77
DIED	January 18, 1970, at Salt Lake City, age 96

"Every member a missionary."

JOSE[PH]

BORN	
MARRIED	
APOSTLE	
PRESIDE[NT]	
DIED	

"This is the [...] f[...]

• **1920–21** First Presidency sends Elder David O. McKay on worldwide tour to visit members and missions

• Primary Children's Hospital opens

TEMPLE 1923
Alberta

• **May** Relief Society sells stored wheat to US to aid war effort of World War I

• **October 3** Joseph F. Smith receives "Vision of the Redemption of the Dead" (D&C 138)

• **October 3** KSL begins radio broadcasts of general conference

• **December 6** Elder Melvin J Ballard opens South America for missionary work

• **Fall** First institute of religion opens, University of Idaho

• **Fall** First seminary opens at Granite High School, Salt Lake City

• Maori Agriculture College, New Zealand, established (destroyed by earth-quake in 1931)

• **May 21** Boy Scouts integrated with YMMIA

• **April** General conference postponed because of influenza epidemic. Held June 1–3

• **January** *Relief Society* magazine founded (until 1970)

• **September** Publication of *Jesus the Christ,* by James E. Talmage

TEMPLE 1919
Hawaii

• **October 2** Church Administration Building completed

TEMPLE 1927
Mesa

• **Ap[ril]** beg[...]
Novemb[er] Washington, D[...] chapel dedica[...]

July 21 Monume[...]

P[...]

a[...]
c[...]

• **July 15** Tabern[acle] begins weekly radio broadcas[t] (later switches [...])

June Richard L Evans begins "Music and the Spoken Word"

• 889 missionaries set apart in 1920

• 896 missionaries set apart in 1930

• 525,987 Church members

• 670,017 Church members

| 1912 | 1914 | 1916 | 1918 | **1920** | 1922 | 1924 | 1926 | 1928 | **1930** | 193[...] |

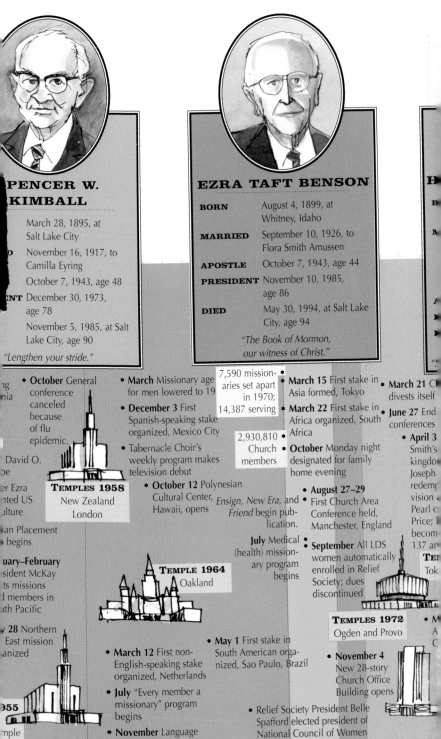

SPENCER W. KIMBALL

March 28, 1895, at
Salt Lake City

November 16, 1917, to
Camilla Eyring

October 7, 1943, age 48

December 30, 1973,
age 78

November 5, 1985, at Salt
Lake City, age 90

"Lengthen your stride."

EZRA TAFT BENSON

BORN	August 4, 1899, at Whitney, Idaho
MARRIED	September 10, 1926, to Flora Smith Amussen
APOSTLE	October 7, 1943, age 44
PRESIDENT	November 10, 1985, age 86
DIED	May 30, 1994, at Salt Lake City, age 94

"The Book of Mormon, our witness of Christ."

- **October** General conference canceled because of flu epidemic.

David O.
be
er Ezra
nted US
ulture

ian Placement
 begins

uary–February
sident McKay
ts missions
d members in
uth Pacific

28 Northern
East mission
anized

955
mple

EMPLE 1956
Los Angeles

- **October 3** Relief Society Building

- 4,706 missionaries set apart in 1960; 9,097 serving

- 1,693,180 Church members

TEMPLES 1958
New Zealand
London

- **March** Missionary age for men lowered to 19
- **December 3** First Spanish-speaking stake organized, Mexico City
- Tabernacle Choir's weekly program makes television debut
- **October 12** Polynesian Cultural Center, Hawaii, opens

TEMPLE 1964
Oakland

- **March 12** First non-English-speaking stake organized, Netherlands
- **July** "Every member a missionary" program begins
- **November** Language Training Institute (Mission) established at BYU

November 1 Southeast Asia Mission opens

- **January** Formal family home evening program inaugurated
- **February** Italy officially reopened to missionary work

7,590 missionaries set apart in 1970; 14,387 serving

2,930,810 Church members

Ensign, New Era, and *Friend* begin publication.

July Medical (health) missionary program begins

- **May 1** First stake in South American organized, Sao Paulo, Brazil

- Relief Society President Belle Spafford elected president of National Council of Women

- **June** First missionaries to Spain

March 8 First stake on mainland Asia organized, Seoul, Korea

- **March 15** First stake in Asia formed, Tokyo
- **March 22** First stake in Africa organized, South Africa
- **October** Monday night designated for family home evening

- **August 27–29** First Church Area Conference held, Manchester, England

- **September** All LDS women automatically enrolled in Relief Society; dues discontinued

TEMPLES 1972
Ogden and Provo

- **November 4** New 28-story Church Office Building opens

- **March 21** C divests itself
- **June 27** End conferences

- **April 3** Smith's kingdo Joseph redemp vision Pearl C Price; l becom 137 an

TE
Tok

- M
A
C

- **February** First agricul sionaries sent to Sout
- **April 7** Welfare Servi Department organize

TEMPL
Washing

1956 1958 **1960** 1962 1964 1966 1968 **1970** 1972 1974 1976

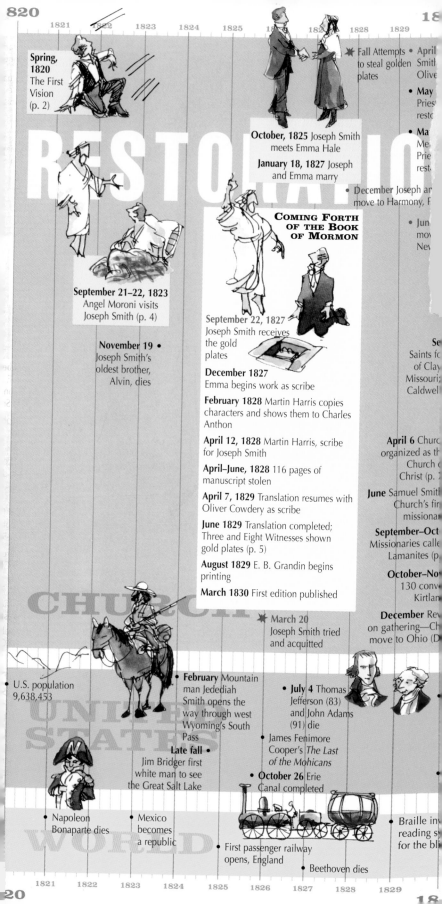

Spring, 1820 The First Vision (p. 2)

October, 1825 Joseph Smith meets Emma Hale

January 18, 1827 Joseph and Emma marry

September 21–22, 1823 Angel Moroni visits Joseph Smith (p. 4)

November 19 • Joseph Smith's oldest brother, Alvin, dies

COMING FORTH OF THE BOOK OF MORMON

September 22, 1827 Joseph Smith receives the gold plates

December 1827 Emma begins work as scribe

February 1828 Martin Harris copies characters and shows them to Charles Anthon

April 12, 1828 Martin Harris, scribe for Joseph Smith

April–June, 1828 116 pages of manuscript stolen

April 7, 1829 Translation resumes with Oliver Cowdery as scribe

June 1829 Translation completed; Three and Eight Witnesses shown gold plates (p. 5)

August 1829 E. B. Grandin begins printing

March 1830 First edition published

Fall Attempts to steal golden plates

• April Smith Olive

• **May** Pries resto

• **Ma** Me Prie rest

• December Joseph ar move to Harmony, F

• Jun mov Nev

Se Saints fo of Clay Missouri Caldwell

April 6 Churc organized as th Church Christ (p.

June Samuel Smith Church's fir missionar

September–Oct Missionaries calle Lamanites (p

October–No 130 conve Kirtlan

December Rev on gathering—Ch move to Ohio (D

March 20 Joseph Smith tried and acquitted

• U.S. population 9,638,453

• **February** Mountain man Jedediah Smith opens the way through west Wyoming's South Pass

Late fall • Jim Bridger first white man to see the Great Salt Lake

• **July 4** Thomas Jefferson (83) and John Adams (91) die

• James Fenimore Cooper's *The Last of the Mohicans*

• **October 26** Erie Canal completed

• Napoleon Bonaparte dies

• Mexico becomes a republic

• First passenger railway opens, England

• Beethoven dies

• Braille inv reading sy for the bli

1831 — 1832 — 1833 — 1834 — 1835 — 1836 — 1837 — 1838 — 1839

Joseph
meets
Cowdery

Aaronic
hood
red (p. 6)

June
hizedek
hood
red (p. 6)

Emma Smith
nnsylvania

Joseph Smith
es to Fayette,
York

February 16
Vision of
degrees
of glory
(D&C
76)

ember
ed out
County,
ttle in
ounty,
issouri

February 1 Joseph
Smith arrives in
Kirtland; Majority of
Saints soon follow

February 4 Edward
Partridge, first bishop

February 9 Law of
consecration (D&C 42)

June 3–6 First high priest
ordained—Elders called to
Missouri (D&C 52)

December Joseph
Smith back in Kirtland

January 25 Joseph
Smith sustained pres-
ident of high priests

March 24 Joseph Smith
and Sidney Rigdon
tarred and feather

June Missionaries
to Canada—first
outside U.S.

January 23 School
of the Prophets
(p. 9)

June 19 Joseph Smith
leaves for Missouri

July 20 Site
for City of Zion
revealed (p. 10)

August 3
Missouri
temple site
dedicated
(p. 10)

November
Book of
Command-
ments
accepted
(p. 9)

February 27
Word of Wisdom
(D&C 89)

March 18 First
Presidency organized

July 23 Kirtland
Temple cornerstone

December 18
Joseph Smith Sr.
first Church patri-
arch (p. 3)

February 17
First high coun-
cil (D&C 102)

May 3 Church
renamed
"The Church
of the Latter-day
Saints" (p. 7)

December 5
Oliver Cowdery
assistant president

September Joseph
returns to Kirtland

May 5 Joseph Smith leads
Zion's Camp (p. 10)

November 7 Saints
forced to flee Jack-
son County

Missouri Persecutions of 1838 (p. 12)

August 6 Election day
fight, Saints forbidden
to vote

October 25 Battle of
Crooked River; David
Patten killed

October 27 Gov. Boggs'
"extermination order"

October 30 Haun's Mill
Massacre

January, 1839 Saints
leave Missouri

February 14 Twelve
apostles chosen (p. 11)

February 28 First Quorum
of Seventy organized

July 6 Mummies
and papyrus pur-
chased (p. 9)

August 17 Doctrine
and Covenants pub-
lished (p. 9)

September 14
Emma Smith directed
to select hymns
(D&C 25)

March 27
Kirtland Temple
dedicated (p. 11)

April 3 Vision of the
Savior, Moses, Elias, and
Elijah (D&C 110)

July 25 Joseph Smith
begins trip in Eastern
states

July 6 Exodus from
Kirtland begins (p. 12)

September 27 Joseph
travels to Missouri

Liberty Jail 1838–1839 (p. 13)

October 31 Joseph
Smith arrested

December 1
Joseph and others impris-
oned in Liberty Jail

March 20–25 Joseph's
epistle to the Saints
(D&C 121–23)

April 16 Joseph escapes
from imprisonment

May 19 Joseph Smith names
Adam-ondi-Ahman

July 20 First
missionaries to
England arrive

July 30 First British
converts (p. 17)

December Joseph
Smith back in Kirtland

November 2 Kirtland Safety
Society Bank

Januar
Missou

Februa
arrive
Illinois

Ma
to N

Novembe
Joseph F.
born, son
Hyrum Sr

January 12 Joseph
Smith moves to
Missouri (p. 12)

March 14 Far We
new Church head
quarters

April Oliver
Cowdery and [
Whitmer excor
nicated (p. 4–5)

April 26 Churc
named "The C
Jesus Christ of
day Saints (p. 7

July 4 Corn
for Far Wes

July 8 Revel
tithing (D&C

August 21
Nate
Turner
leads
slave
upris-
ing in
Virginia

October Cherokee
Indians' "Trail of Tears"

December 7 First
white women cross
continent to Oregon
territory

March/April
Texas indepen-
dence from
Mexico

Financial panic
throughout U.S.

Abne
create
base

dediah
ith leads
st covered
agons into
ocky
ountains

.S. population
2,866,020

ts
em

**French
Foreign
Legion
created**

Hans Christian
Anderson publishes
fairy tales

**Victoria becomes
queen of the
United Kingdom**

Bicyc
in Sc

FIELDING ITH

... 19, 1876, at
Lake City

... 26, 1898, to Louie
...liff (died March 30,
...3)

... ember 2, 1908, to Ethel
...olds (died August 26,
...7)

... 12, 1938, to Jessie
...s Smith

... 7, 1910, age 33

... ary 23, 1970, age 93

... 2, 1972, at Salt Lake
... age 95

*...arning. . . . Be true and
... all things."*

HAROLD B. LEE

BORN	March 28, 1899, at Clifton, Idaho
MARRIED	November 14, 1923, to Fern Tanner (died September 24, 1962) June 17, 1963, to Freda J. Jensen
APOSTLE	April 10, 1941, age 42
PRESIDENT	July 7, 1972, age 73
DIED	December 26, 1973, at Salt Lake City, age 74

"Priesthood, the strength of the Church."

S...

BORN	
MARRI...	
APOSTL...	
PRESID...	
DIED	

*...eret News
...rch News"*

January 28 San •
Diego Mormon
Battalion Monument
dedicated

1,194 •
missionaries set
apart in 1940

...norah •
...cated

... 7 Church •
(Welfare)
...ntroduced

862,664 •
Church
members

January Ages •
...nic Priesthood
...ent adopted—
...2; teacher, 15;
priest, 17

July First Hill •
...morah Pageant

...mmer President •
...Heber J. Grant
tours Europe
...ir

August 14 •
First Deseret
Industries
opens

June 19 Liberty Jail •
purchased for Church

August 24 Missionaries •
in Germany moved to
neutral countries

October First •
public television
broadcast of
general
conference

March 23 During •
war only older
men called on full-
time missions

April During war, •
conference atten-
dance restricted to
General Authorities
and stake presiden-
cies—Tabernacle
closed for duration
of war

March 7 First •
Indian-only mission
formed, Navaho-
Zuni Mission

September •
Mission presidents
sent to areas aban-
doned during the war

October Tabernacle •
reopened

December Number •
of yearly visitors to
Temple Square
reaches 1 million

Church sends material aid •
to Saints in Europe

July 24 Celebration •
of 100th anniversary
of pioneers' arrival in
valley

1,016,170 •
Church
members

August 31 Aaronic •
Priesthood age ad-
vancement approved:
teacher, age 14; priest
age 16

July Church •
Building Committee
organized

August 17 Southern •
Far East mission
organized

TEMPLE 1945
Idaho Falls

September First early mor... •
seminaries, Southern Calif...

3,015 missionaries •
set apart in 1950

1,111,314 Church membe... •

Summer Preside... •
McKay tours Eur...

November 25 El... •
Taft Benson appo...
Secretary of Agric...

July Ind... •
Progra...

Ja... •
Pr...
vi...
an...
So...

Ju... •
Fa...
or...

TEMPL...
Swiss, fi...
European...